Cricket in Chesterfield

*A Century of Club
and County Matches
at Queen's Park*

Janet Murphy

MERTON

First published 2008

Published by
Merton Priory Press Ltd
9 Owen Falls Avenue
Chesterfield S41 0FR

For the Friends of Queen's Park

ISBN 978 1 898937 73 9

Printed by
Dinefwr Press Ltd
Rawlings Road, Llandybie
Carmarthenshire SA18 3YD

Contents

Preface

Mention Queen's Park, Chesterfield, to many people and they immediately think of cricket. Home of Chesterfield Cricket Club, the ground has hosted teams at all levels from schoolchildren to international touring sides.

This short history of cricket in Queen's Park is a companion volume to *For the People of Chesterfield For Ever: a short history of Queen's Park*, published by Merton for the Friends of Queen's Park in 2006.

The section relating to matches played at Queen's Park by Derbyshire County Cricket Club after 1946 is based substantially upon the recollections of events by players, spectators and officials. For more detailed information about the matches readers are referred to the *Derbyshire County Cricket Club Year Book* which has been produced annually since 1954. The volume for 2006 contained detailed statistics of the first-class matches at Queen's Park, an updated version of which may be obtained from David Baggett, who may be contacted through Derbyshire County Cricket Club. Information about earlier games may be found in the *Derbyshire Cricket Guide 1886–1939*, the *Derbyshire Times* and the *Derbyshire Courier. The History of Derbyshire County Cricket Club* by John Shawcroft places the matches at Chesterfield in the context of the history of the club as does *Cricket Grounds of Derbyshire* by the same author. Noëlle McCarroll's *Chesterfield Cricket Club: 100 Years at Queen's Park* provides additional information about Chesterfield Cricket Club.

A list of the contributors of recollections and photographs will be found at the end of the text. I am grateful to you all, they have enriched the book.

I have had a great deal of additional help from a lot of people, especially Brian Austin, who told me about Thomas Hunt, the members of Chesterfield Cricket Club, in particular the chairman, Mike Taylor, the scorer and honorary secretary, Steve Franks, and Noëlle McCarroll, who gave me permission to quote from her book *Chesterfield Cricket Club: 100 Years at Queen's Park*; Derbyshire County Cricket Club, in particular David Baggett, who gave me permission to quote from the *Derbyshire County Cricket Club Yearbooks* and read the text for me, and the staff of Chesterfield Local Studies Library and of Chesterfield Museum and Art Gallery. Wherever possible permission to publish photographs has been obtained from the owners of the copyright, including the editors of *Derbyshire Life and Countryside,* the *Derbyshire Times,* and Sheffield Newspapers, together with Neil Robinson of the MCC Library.

Profits from the book will be divided between the Friends of Queen's Park and Chesterfield Cricket Club.

1 The early history of cricket in Chesterfield

Cricket in North Derbyshire has a long history. William Cavendish, 3rd duke of Devonshire, whose Derbyshire home was at Chatsworth, played cricket in Hyde Park in 1730 and the *Derby Mercury* in 1757 recorded a match at Brampton Moor, just outside Chesterfield, between teams from Sheffield and Wirksworth. It seems likely that cricket was also being played in Chesterfield at this time, although the early history of cricket in the town is not well documented.

The first of a series of articles about the history of cricket in Chesterfield, which appeared in the *Derbyshire Courier* during August 1914, said that the earliest reference to cricket in the town was to a match played at the time of the construction of the Chesterfield Canal in the 1770s when:

> The navvies engaged in constructing the new cut left their shovels and spades to watch the gentlemen playing, nor would they return to their work again that day, so interested were they to see which side would win the wager.

In 1783 Chesterfield played Sheffield at Brampton Moor, but this does not mean that Chesterfield Cricket Club has had a continual existence from this date. During the next hundred years there were several different clubs in the town, most of which had only a brief existence.

The presence of wagers ensured that these early games were fiercely contested. About 1812 a game was played by the gentlemen of the town on land between Newbold Lane and Saltergate (later occupied by the Union Workhouse). The match was interrupted by the constable with a message from the court house requesting the presence of three of the team members, 'as the business of the court could not go on without them'. One of the men was the town clerk, Mr Waller, who sent a message back to the mayor that he should announce the court adjourned for the day as all the required gentlemen were 'already too far spent in their exertions in upholding the honour of the town on the cricket field to attend decently to the duties of the court house'.

In 1823 the primary club in the town was the North Derbyshire Cricket Club, with a membership exceeding 40, and whose annual ball and supper was a notable event in the area, which suggests it was a club for the gentry. Another early club was the Albion.

During the 1830s and 1840s Chesterfield had a strong side. Initially their ground was on Derby Lane (now Derby Road). The matches were great social occasions and, when important games were to be played and wagers were particularly high, several tents would be erected on the ground decorated with the club colours. The players wore white flannel jackets with outside pockets and white flannel trousers, both trimmed with blue. Chesterfield Cricket Club was in existence at this time as the club badge bore the initials CCC.

The star of the period was Thomas Hunt. Born in Chesterfield in 1819 he was apprenticed to a coach builder, but spent all his spare time playing cricket. When his apprenticeship was finished, he became a professional cricketer with the Sheffield Club before moving to the Manchester Club. These were the forerunners of the Yorkshire and Lancashire sides. He also played for Yorkshire, Lancashire, the North of England and once for the Players. When he was 39 he died from his injuries after being hit by a train at Rochdale. Chesterfield has produced some fine all-rounders, most notably the Pope brothers, Geoff Miller and Ian Blackwell; but Thomas Hunt was possibly the most complete all-round cricketer of them all; as well as batting and bowling on pitches which were under-prepared, he also kept wicket on several

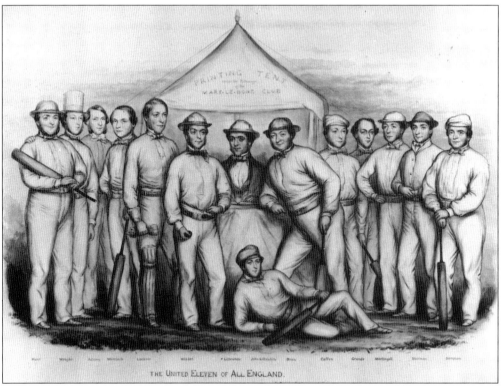

1. The United Eleven of All England. *From left to right:* T. Hunt, G.H. Wright, T.M. Adams, W. Mortlock, T. Lockyer, J. Wisden, F. Lillywhite, J. Dean, W. Caffyn, J. Grundy, W. Martingell, T. Sherman, H. Sampson. *In front:* J. Lillywhite. (© MCC Photo Library)

occasions. Records survive for 39 first-class matches in which he took part over 13 seasons. He scored 922 runs at an average of 15.11, took 67 wickets at an average of 14.94, and made 33 catches and nine stumpings. He augmented his income by playing single- and double-wicket matches. In 1845 he played a Knaresborough XI. Hunt scored 23 and ten but Knaresborough only managed 16 and nine and 14 of those were wides! He was known as the Star of the North.

When Chesterfield played Derby in 1845 Derby refused to play if Hunt was in the Chesterfield side. The first game resulted in victory for Chesterfield, the Derby club having left for home on the second day because of the wet weather 'without bidding their opponents a "good bye" or saying that they had given the match up.' Annoyed that Derby had included several first-rate cricketers from other clubs, Chesterfield insisted on playing Hunt in the return game, which resulted in a defeat for Derby by eight wickets. Man of the match was undoubtedly Hunt who bowled five batsmen, stumped one, and scored 56 not out of a total of 115. On the scorecard if the batsman was caught, the fielder was credited with the wicket, but not the bowler, so Hunt may have taken more wickets.

The ground at Derby Lane had to be given up because an embankment was built across it during the construction of the Midland Railway. The development of a railway network enabled the formation of itinerant elevens, the earliest of which was the All England XI, which toured the country playing exhibition games against local sides which had as many as 22 players. Hunt played for the rival United All England XI. These games were undertaken with the intention of increasing the popularity of the game. Conversely in Chesterfield the interest in cricket declined, probably because there was no permanent cricket ground and, in 1856, only one match was played on the militia drill ground on Saltergate, another ground on Wheeldon Lane having been given up because of a shortage of funds.

In order to raise money to pay the ground rental and playing expenses members paid subscriptions and clubs also charged admission to matches. One of the biggest problems facing a town cricket club was the lack of a suitable ground. Wheeldon Lane was described as 'insalubrious' and 'disrespectable', which no doubt deterred many spectators and discouraged the gentry from playing there, although their money was necessary to keep the club in existence. At a meeting early in 1857, two clubs were formed, the Devonshire on the drill ground on Saltergate and the Albion on Wheeldon Lane. A year later both clubs were playing on the drill ground, and there was immense excitement when 22 of Derby and District (including Thomas Hunt) played an All England XI; Derby and District winning by 12 wickets. There were still more changes the following year when two different teams were formed, Chesterfield United and Scarsdale. Members of the Scarsdale Club were all amateur and, with a subscription of £1, mostly gentry. It lasted for just one

2. Chesterfield from the south in 1849. The house on the left is West House, the home of the Maynard family and the fields opposite were known as Maynard's Meadows. The lane in the centre is Wheeldon Lane and the figures are taking part in a cricket match. (Chesterfield Library Local Studies)

year. The secretary of Chesterfield United was T.P. Wood so it can be assumed that the United Club evolved into the Chesterfield Cricket Club as he was associated with the latter club until his death. The club began playing on the (Old) Recreation Ground on Saltergate (Tennyson Avenue was later built on the site), but soon moved to a ground at Broad Oaks before going back to Wheeldon Lane, although when a second All England match was arranged in 1861 it was played on the Recreation Ground.

In the *Derbyshire Courier* of 19 October 1867 it was announced that the committee of the Chesterfield Cricket Club had great pleasure in informing their friends that during the winter months they intended to open a football club. Subscriptions were set at 1s. 0d. for members of the Cricket Club and 2s. 6d. for non-members. The advertisement was evidently successful as, on 19 February 1868, Chesterfield Football Club played its first match at the (Old) Recreation Ground, Saltergate, and Chesterfield Cricket Club returned to the ground. Also in 1868 the first Chesterfield Athletic Sports event, organised by the Cricket Club, was held on Whit Monday. The events became very popular and attracted big crowds, providing the club with a much needed income

However relations between the Cricket Club and the owner of the Recreation Ground were not harmonious and in 1871, following a dispute over the use of the ground, the club decided to find a new home. They rented the two fields which lay between Saltergate and Cobden Road, with just one field between the Old and the New Recreation Grounds, which must have caused some confusion. The Football Club and the athletics events went with them. The Cricket Club immediately advertised for local publicans who would be prepared to serve refreshments on the ground and for local butchers and graziers, who had flocks of sheep to graze on the ground. Chesterfield Cricket Club played their first game there on 7 June 1871. The highlights of the season were a match with Yorkshire and the visit of the United South of England Cricket Team, including the brothers G.F. and W.G. Grace, who played against 22 of Chesterfield & District. About the same time the cricket and football clubs developed separate administrations and became separate clubs.

In 1881 Chesterfield Football Club was wound up because of an alarming deficit and the success of another local side, the Spital Football Club, which became the premier club in the town, playing teams such as Sheffield Wednesday and West Bromwich and therefore attracting the spectators. Chesterfield Football Club was re-formed in 1884.

During the 1870s and early 1880s Chesterfield Cricket Club was a strong side. At least ten members of the club also represented Derbyshire. Although most only played a few times, William Mycroft was the leading Derbyshire bowler of the time; E.A.J. Maynard captained Derbyshire from 1885 to 1887; and other notable players were William Cropper and Frederick Keeton, together with H.R.J. Charlwood who played for Sussex and was in W.G. Grace's side in 1871.

However in March 1887 the *Derbyshire Courier* reported that the Cricket Club had given up the ground at Saltergate and that the old pavilion and grandstand were being demolished. The Football Club remained in existence.

With too few members and a diminishing number of spectators at the matches there was insufficient income to meet the club's outgoings. There were several contributory factors to the declining interest in the club, including the poor playing surface, the growth of professional sport, and the proliferation of works and village teams. Almost twenty years after the first athletics event the cost of providing prizes and appearance money for the competitions was now draining money from the club. The formation of Derbyshire County Cricket Club in 1870 attracted professional players like William Mycroft and William Cropper. Brimington Cricket club was the outstanding team of the time. Founded in 1884 they won the Derbyshire Challenge Cup in 1887, in its inaugural season, as well as in 1888 and they were semi-finalists in 1889. It was a strong side. Living in Brimington at the time were the Davidson brothers, George and Frank, the Mycroft half-brothers, William and Thomas, and the Cropper brothers, William and Martin: all but Martin Cropper played for Derbyshire; he played for the Second Eleven. Other strong teams were Sheepbridge and Staveley; these local sides attracted the spectators and support for Chesterfield declined. The remaining players and the committee moved to the Parish Church Cricket Club. T.P. Wood, however, remained aloof.

It was agreed to commemorate the golden jubilee of Queen Victoria in 1887 by raising funds to purchase land for a public recreation ground for the people of Chesterfield. An appeal was launched for £4,000 in order to buy two fields south of the river Hipper together with a further £250 for land for a roadway from West Bars. The land was owned by E.A.J. Maynard, captain of Derbyshire at the time. Money was collected slowly, but by August sufficient had been promised for the Jubilee Committee to decide to go ahead with the purchase of the larger 17-acre field for £3,000 and the land for the roadway. The first plans for the Park did not include a cricket ground as an appeal had immediately been launched for the £1,000 to purchase the second five-acre field for cricket. Again progress was slow, but enough money was raised to purchase the land in 1889, thanks to the efforts of the ladies of the town who organised a five-day bazaar at the Stephenson Memorial Hall.

In 1889 an attempt was made to form a tradesmen's team following the adoption of Wednesday as half-day closing in the town, but instead it was decided to re-form the old Chesterfield Cricket Club, which would play on the (New) Recreation Ground again. Although the Derbyshire League was founded in 1889, Chesterfield did not join until 1893, by which time some of the more talented players had returned to the club and at last there was the prospect of a properly laid-out cricket ground.

2 Cricket in Queen's Park 1894–1945

Queen's Park was officially opened in August 1893, but the cricket ground was not used until the following season. The council maintained the ground. In January a set of leather shoes was purchased for the horse drawing the large roller on the cricket ground. In February the Parks Committee met to lay down the rules for the cricket ground. The Chesterfield Town Cricket Club was granted the privilege of playing on the ground upon payment of half the annual subscription per member providing that the subscription was not less than 10s. and only members could practice and play in matches. For Junior Clubs (i.e. clubs other than Chesterfield) the charge was 2s. 6d. per member. Persons other than members could play on application to the Parks Committee at 10s. 6d. per match.

The cost of the subscription deterred the working classes from joining the Chesterfield Cricket Club and a deputation to the Council asked that the cost for working men should be 2s. 6d. A compromise was reached that 5s. should be the cost for half the members and 2s. 6d. for the rest. In April Chesterfield Cricket Club decided to move to the Park and a pavilion was transferred from the Old Recreation Ground. The first match, a friendly, was played on 5 May 1894 between Chesterfield and Clay Cross, and resulted in a heavy defeat for Clay Cross. The first Derbyshire League match was on 19 May, which Ilkeston won easily. The first victory came on 16 June at the expense of Morton, a team Chesterfield played many times over succeeding years. Before the end of the season, the first century had been scored by B. Storer and the first hat-trick performed by Boam. In their first season in Queen's Park Chesterfield played 18 matches in the Derbyshire League, winning nine, losing eight and drawing one. They finished in the middle of the table. One player who missed several matches was the all-rounder George Walker who was playing for Derbyshire. George Davidson, son of Joe Davidson (a Chesterfield stalwart for many years), was his contemporary. Another all-rounder, George Davidson was the third cricketer after W. G. Grace and W. Flowers to achieve the double and his innings of 274 against Lancashire in 1896 is still the highest innings for Derbyshire. Sadly he died of pneumonia in 1899 at the early age of 32. Although primarily a Brimington player he played a few games for Chesterfield.

The move to the Park did not solve the financial problems. The club was £45 10s. 6d. in debt and the cost of playing in the Park was ten guineas. At the Recreation Ground the club had been able to charge admission to matches; they were not allowed to do this in the Park, but made collections around the ground which raised about £5. The Parks Committee had paid £10 for the hire of the horse used for rolling and mowing the ground and paid the wages of the park keeper and his assistant to get the ground ready. The committee was unhappy as it had expected the club to have more members and therefore have to pay a higher sum for the use of the cricket ground. Alderman T.P. Wood thought a town the size of Chesterfield should have a club with 400 members; as it was they had 65 members and he had paid the subscriptions of half of them. He complained about the 'curse of cricket' which brought headlines in the local press and caused consternation in the cricket club. However he was not referring to the game itself, but to the growth of cup and league cricket which meant that directly a young player showed signs of being a good player, he expected to be paid his day's wage if he played and his expenses if the match was away, instead of playing for the love of the game. In those days of long working hours and low wages it seems reasonable that the working men of the club should be paid their expenses, but it possibly placed Chesterfield at a financial disadvantage compared with sides from local works, whose owner probably employed the players and provided the ground.

A year later the club was £30 in debt, had to tender to play on the ground, and was not allowed to make collections. However they had a successful start to their time in the Derbyshire League, winning it in 1896 and finishing second in 1898 and 1899.

3. The pavilion was erected in 1898 in time for the first county match. (Chesterfield Museum and Art Gallery)

From the start, the pitch was recognised as excellent and thoughts turned to having representative matches on the ground, Derbyshire having been given first-class status again in 1894. In 1897 Chesterfield Cricket Club applied for the Park to be closed for three days the following season for a county match, free of charge to the club who would make their own arrangements for the preparation of the ground. First however a new pavilion was required, which was opened by the mayor on 28 April, just in time for the new season. The cost was £499 18s. 6d.

The first County Championship match at Queen's Park was played on 30 June, 1 and 2 July 1898. Although Derbyshire were heavily defeated by Surrey, the match was a commercial success, and Walter Sugg asked for his benefit match against Yorkshire to be transferred to Chesterfield. The result was Derbyshire's heaviest defeat ever as the Yorkshire openers amassed 554 runs in 305 minutes out of a total of 662. However Derbyshire did not have the best of luck. George Davidson broke down after bowling only one over. By the time they batted the pitch was described as 'worn' and they were soon dismissed for 118. Following on they were 50 for one at the close of play with Frank Davidson not out 5. Despite the fact that Derbyshire were still 494 behind almost a thousand spectators turned up for the final day's play. Unfortunately Davidson had to retire on 5 because he had to go to Dudley to play in a club match; Charlesworth was unable to bat because of a broken finger and G. Davidson and Chatterton were 'lame'. The match had a farcical finish. When the luncheon bell rang the players left the field but, as the Derbyshire last-wicket pair were at the crease, the players decided to return to the middle with the idea of bringing the game to a swift conclusion. However Walker and Ashcroft defended stubbornly and eventually lunch was taken with them still undefeated, only for the match to finish with the first ball after lunch. Sugg made £340 from the match. The *Derbyshire Times* recounted the work involved in connection with the match:

> The number of Press and ordinary work in connection with the County match reached the enormous total of 5,000 messages, the Press totalling 63,000 words which is a record for the county. Although the local staff was reinforced by four telegraphists from Derby, in the charge of Mr Elks, and a Wheatstone transmitter, the pressure of work was so heavy that none of the men were able to leave the building from 11 a.m. to 9 p.m. and it is pleasing to be able to state that every item was disposed of in admirable time, the wants of the inner man being sacrificed to duty.

At the end of the season the club paid £25 to the Corporation as a goodwill gesture as the matches had been so profitable.

In October 1898 Chesterfield Cricket Club applied to have exclusive use of

4. The Derbyshire team for the match against Surrey. *Standing:* J. Wheeler (umpire), W. Storer, J. Wright, W.B. Delacombe (Secretary), J.W. Hancock, W.J. Piper (Hon. Scorer), H. Bagshaw, W. Bestwick, M. Sherwin (umpire) *Seated:* G.A. Davidson, W. Sugg, W. Chatterton, S.H. Evershed (Captain), W. Boden (President), G.G. Walker, L.G. Wright. (*T.P. Wood's Almanac 1899*)

the ground and pavilion with power to allow the use by other cricket clubs in the borough. For the privilege, the club would pay the Corporation £20 a year and be entitled to receive a subscription from other clubs. They undertook to keep the ground in order, without any claim on the Corporation. Permission was granted provided that the subscribing clubs did not lose their identity. They also had to pay for the days the Park was closed for cricket; the Corporation wanted £30 per first-class match, but reduced the fee to £25 on appeal.

The first double-century for Derbyshire (at Chesterfield) came in their fourth match on the ground when W. Storer scored 216 not out against Leicestershire. He might well have scored more as he was on 216 overnight, but when play started the following morning, the other not-out batsman, Bestwick, was not on the ground and the innings closed. A collection for Storer raised £6 10s. The first victory came against Worcestershire in 1900.

From the start, events in the Park were hugely popular and, in 1900, a terrace was built to the west of the pavilion at a cost of £264 8s. 6d. Seating was provided — planks of wood on iron supports. This also meant that cricket clubs could charge admission to the terrace and pavilion. Admission to enclosure was set at 2d., to be shared out amongst the cricket clubs.

In 1901 there was a rebate of £10 owing to unfavourable weather and diminution of gate receipts. In 1908 a further £75 was remitted to the club

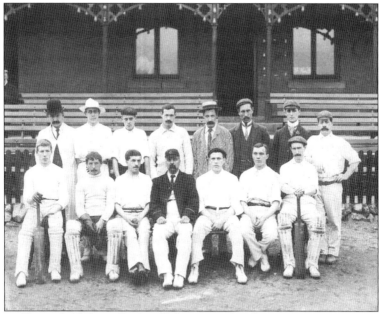

5. Chesterfield Town Cricket Club in 1902. *Standing:* F. Gaston, W. Brunlees, F. Tattersall, J. Harvey, G. Tattersall, P. Evans, E. Holland. *Seated:* L. Hartley, W. Mellon, W. Wray, S. Cook (Captain), G. Pearce, T. Sawyer, S. Cantrell. (Chesterfield Museum and Art Gallery)

because of bad weather. The following year the agreement was £10 per match, £10 for the ground and no rebate. About this time the future of the County Club was in doubt as the committee stated that 'Owing to the present position, both from a financial and a playing point of view, the question now arises as to the advisability of continuing the Club'. One suggestion was that the club should relocate to Queen's Park, but there were felt to be too many drawbacks to a scheme to enlarge the Park and instead the suggestion was made that a new cricket ground should be established opposite the Terminus Hotel at Brampton.

W.G. Grace played at Queen's Park on two occasions, in 1901 and 1904, playing for London County. The 1901 game was ruined by the weather; Grace was run out for nought and took nought for 15. Three years later he did somewhat better, scoring 37 and taking nine for 160 in the match, but was unable to prevent Derbyshire winning by 139 runs.

In 1904 there was a most remarkable match:

> I sat next to a retired gentleman, who was in his eighties ... The most important memory he had and conveyed to me was that he had been a Derbyshire supporter all his life and he had been present at the first match in the Park in 1898 when Derbyshire played Surrey. He said that at the time the pavilion was just the bit in the middle; the two gable-end portions were added later. In 1904

6. W.G. Grace takes guard. The building in the background stood on the embankment of the Lancashire, Derbyshire & East Coast Railway. (Chesterfield Museum and Art Gallery)

Essex batted first and scored 597 with Perrin making 343 not out. Derbyshire batted and reached 548 before lunch on the third and final day and a draw appeared likely. However Essex were dismissed for 97 and Derbyshire required 147 in just 125 minutes. They reached the total with 45 minutes to spare. The retired gentleman had been there and it was his greatest memory of the Park. (Ken Silcock)

7. The players leave the field after the match. C.A. Ollivierre is the third player from the left. (D. Tyler)

The undoubted batting hero for Derbyshire was the West Indian C.A. Ollivierre with 229 (including a five) and 92 not out. 229 remains the highest score for a Derbyshire player at Chesterfield. Bestwick and Warren took 13 wickets between them. Perrin's 343* remains the highest score by any batsman finishing on the losing side. Amazingly, of the four occasions in international cricket that a batsman has scored a triple-century and finished on the losing side, two of the innings have been against Derbyshire; the 312 scored by Jason Gallian for Lancashire against Derbyshire at Old Trafford in 1996 being the other.

The matches were not always high scoring as Derbyshire were routed for 32 by Nottinghamshire in 1904, 36 (and 80) by Leicestershire in 1905 and 37 (and 78) by Kent in 1907.

As early as 1914 the *Derbyshire Courier* said that Chesterfield had been the venue of many remarkable matches; it then reported a sensational ending to the match with Yorkshire as Derbyshire collapsed from 67 for four to 68 all out. Arthur Morton, who opened the innings, scored 50 and was the last out. Six batsmen did not trouble the scorers and, for Yorkshire, Drake took five wickets for six runs including four wickets in four balls and Rhodes four wickets for 12. The writer put it down to Yorkshire's good luck as Derbyshire had had the worst of the batting conditions.

During the First World War most able-bodied men went into the Forces and there was only a small military presence in the town. With few members, Chesterfield Cricket Club was disbanded in 1915, a fate which befell many other clubs. Matches were held to raise funds for the British Red Cross and, in 1917, Markham & Company played the Tube Works to raise funds for the tradesmen's appeal for the Chesterfield & North Derbyshire Hospital.

Once the armistice was signed in November 1918, thoughts again turned to cricket. On 30 January 1919, sixteen gentlemen attended a meeting at the Station Hotel when it was proposed to restart the Chesterfield Cricket Club. The first task was to try to reduce the overdraft of £83 at the bank and it was decided to hold a concert to raise funds. In 1919 the First Eleven played in the Derbyshire League, the Second Eleven rejoined the Derbyshire Minor Cricket League and the Wednesday Team competed for the Eyre Challenge Cup on a knock-out basis, a competition which they won.

The president of the club was Colonel John Morton Clayton, who had first played for the club in 1876, played for Derbyshire in 1881 and 1883 and had taken part in the first match on the ground. He and his brother Joseph, who also played for Chesterfield, were the sons of James Clayton who had established Clayton's Tannery in Chesterfield in 1840. The company is still in existence today and amongst its products is the leather which has been used for the manufacture of cricket balls the world over.

Permission was sought from the Parks Committee to erect a memorial to cricketers killed during the war. Little is known of Gerald Stanway, other than

8. The Roll of Honour in the cricket pavilion. (Janet Murphy)

that he is listed on the Chesterfield Roll of Honour. Of the other ten men listed on the memorial five were old boys of Chesterfield Grammar School. Of these only two have cricket mentioned in their obituaries, Charles Newcombe, who played for Derbyshire against Yorkshire in 1910, and Harry Peach, who was described as a promising cricketer. Another, Herbert Lack, played both for the Grammar School and for Chesterfield Cricket Club. The other two old boys, William Jacques and Tom Black, seem no longer to have been interested in cricket. Of the others Tom Bennett played for the Chesterfield Corporation Employees Club; William Ford, an employee of Crompton & Evans Bank, played for Chesterfield Cricket Club Wednesday side; and Frank Stinchcombe and Joseph Millward played for Chesterfield Cricket Club. Although Colin Godwin played for Chesterfield Cricket Club he was better known in Clowne, where he captained the town team and also played football for Clowne Town.

After the First World War a Sports Committee was formed to promote sport across the borough and to develop the Park Annexe. The Parks Committee was responsible for allocating and maintaining areas in the parks and recreation grounds for sporting activities, which they then rented out to the Sports Committee, which in turn was responsible for the organisation of the matches. Needless to say there was much confusion, with the Cricket Club applying to both committees for permission to arrange a county match. Some councillors served on both committees and it is difficult to see why the Sports Committee was responsible for arranging band concerts.

There were problems with the employment of a groundsman, principally because the club could only afford to pay for the weeks of the cricket season, usually from the end of March until the end of September.

In 1919 Isaac Middleton was employed part-time for £1 a week. The following year he was employed full-time from 12 April until 13 September at £3 a week. However he engaged himself to the Football Club on 20 August and went to work for them for several days a week. The following season the Cricket Club had to wait until May before he could begin. From 1922 his wages were augmented by the payment of expenses involved in the preparation of the ground for the county matches, paid by the County Club.

As well as maintaining the ground, the club was also responsible for the catering arrangements during matches, the provision and removal of extra seating at county matches and the employment of gatemen. They also had to pay the Corporation for the days the Park was closed for cricket matches. Income came from subscriptions and a percentage of the gate receipts from the County Club, which was often late in paying. No wonder that the club was frequently overdrawn. It continued to be responsible for the arrangements for the use of the ground by clubs as diverse as the Tube Works, Chesterfield Butchers, Holywell Cross Primitive Methodist Chapel, Chesterfield Grammar School and the County Police.

Derbyshire went through a difficult period after the war; in 1920 one match at Chesterfield was abandoned, the rest were lost. Unfortunately for Joe Humphries the abandoned match, which was against Nottinghamshire, should have been his benefit match — fortunately he was insured. Chesterfield Cricket Club was frequently asked to contribute money raised by events such as whist drives to the County Club's funds.

By 1921 the pavilion was reported to be in a dilapidated state. Three years later the borough surveyor was requested to provide 'plans and estimates for substitution of glass for the slate verandah roof and increasing the seating thereunder'. There is no indication that this was ever carried out — it would surely have been very dangerous to sit there!

When the Park was originally opened in 1893 the bye-laws only allowed it to be closed for 12 days in a year. By 1923 there were five county cricket matches being played and the Park was also being closed for the flower show and sports such as cycling and athletics. To regularise the position a clause in the Chesterfield Corporation Bill of that year (which sought to extend the boundaries of the borough) included a proposal that the Corporation should be able to close the Park for 24 days a year. In support it was stated that:

> The County Cricket Club look to Chesterfield for the main support of the county. They get more out of Chesterfield than all the other parts of the county put together, and more is taken at Chesterfield in one match than in three at Derby.

A new groundsman, G. W. Chapman, was appointed for 1925 at £4 per week for 26 weeks plus 10s. per day extra for the supervision of the ground on Sundays during county matches; however the wages now covered the preparation of the ground for county matches, the expenses being paid to Chesterfield Cricket Club. On 11 August he was dismissed by telegram because of his continual absence from duties. It could have been no surprise that he was finding the daily journey from Stoke almost impossible. A young

George Pope had been employed as his assistant at 15s. per week.

Harry Williams was appointed in 1926 and asked for £4 10s. a week for 52 weeks, but he had to accept £4 from March to September. He stayed for three seasons before leaving at the end of October 1928 for Dulwich in south London. Possibly he was not happy in the south of England because he became groundsman at Derby following the retirement of Albert Widdowson in August 1930. His replacement was J. (Tinker) Simpson, at £3 10s. a week from March 1929. Two years later his wages were raised to £3 15s. In March 1932 he refused to sign a new contract for the following season unless he was paid a sum to include winter months. The club could only offer £2 10s. a week for the full year, but Simpson would accept nothing less than £3. As he had been offered a post as permanent groundsman on the playing fields of the Grammar School and the Girls' High School, it was decided to advertise for a new groundsman.

Fred Pope was appointed at £3 a week, but by July he was being accused of lack of care of tackle, ignorance of how to prepare pitches and being incapable of taking instruction from the county groundsman. He was given a second chance, possibly because his sons, including George Pope, were playing for the club. He was dismissed in September. Possibly there was a clash of personalities as he went on to a successful career at Edgbaston. In his place the club decided to retain the assistant Walter Goodyear, who had been employed as a groundsman's boy two years earlier, when aged just 14, under Tinker Simpson. His wages were £1 1s. a week, probably because of his youth, and the county groundsman, Williams, was to be approached to advise on the preparation of the county pitches. Goodyear moved to Derby in time for the 1938 season and remained there until he retired in 1982.

9. The scorecard for the match against the Australians in 1930. (Cricket New South Wales)

The Australians visited Chesterfield for the first time in 1926. Arrangements for the match included a temporary enclosure (admission 2s.), a press tent furnished with two tables costing 8s. each, an R.A.C. man to direct traffic and white rosettes for the committee members. Despite the 2s. gate money and poor weather there was a crowd of several thousand on each of the two days.

The Australian scorer on the tours in 1926, 1930 and 1934 was Bill Ferguson. He was a talented artist and decorated his scorebooks with small drawings of grounds where the Australians played. The 1930 scorebook had illustrations of the pavilion and of the bandstand.

The Australian press was not impressed with the performance of their team on that tour. C.G. Macartney of the *Evening News* wrote:

> It was a poor exhibition of bowling. ... There was a lack of life about the fielding, while returns to the wicket were awkward and erratic. ... The Australians did not show to advantage in strategy in this game, nor was the batting, in most cases, impressive.

Despite this critical report Australia won by ten wickets. For Derbyshire, Worthington scored 75 in 125 minutes and followed it with four for 103 including Ponsford, Jackson and Bradman, the latter's batting was described as 'scratchy'! He made up for it four years later when he made an elegant 71.

In 1929 the Corporation spent £105 on repairing and renovating the central portion of the pavilion. At the same time the pavilion was greatly extended thanks to the generosity of Alderman G.A. Eastwood, the club's president and a past player. Additional changing-rooms were added at either side with office space above, and two small balconies. The balconies were made into one long one in 1953, but no major changes were made to the layout until the restoration in 2001.

Expenses increased as ground rental rose from £30 to £50 and the share of the county gate was reduced from 15 per cent to 10 per cent.

However it was a successful period for Chesterfield Cricket Club. The First Eleven won the Derbyshire League in 1923 and a year later the Derbyshire League Challenge Cup. In 1928 the Second Eleven joined the newly formed second division of the Derbyshire League. Two years later they won the title helped by 19-year-old George Pope who headed the batting (29.20) and bowling averages (26 wickets at 6.69). Both elevens regularly finished in the top six of their respective leagues; the First Eleven won the Rayner Cup in 1934 and 1935 and the Second Eleven won Division 2 in 1938.

The Pope family's involvement with Chesterfield Cricket Club started when Fred Pope (father of Alf, Eric, George, Harold and Jack) came to Chesterfield in 1913. He was an all-rounder who played in the First Eleven in 1919. Alf, George and Harry all played cricket for Derbyshire and they appeared together in a match against the West Indians at Derby in 1939. Unfortunately the careers of the three brothers were badly affected by the war.

10. The cartoon celebrating Chesterfield Cricket Club as Derbyshire League Champions 1923. (*T.P. Wood's Almanac 1924*)

One game for Chesterfield which stood out in George's memory was a match against Beighton, when, although only 15-years-old, he scored 77 and took 8 for 12. He was presented with a bat after this achievement. He made his debut for the Derbyshire team at Queen's Park in 1933 when he scored 32 and helped Worthington (200*) add 91 for the sixth wicket. The following year he was made an honorary member of Chesterfield Cricket Club, but as he was a professional, it was decided that he could not win any prizes. However, when he headed the first team batting (68.60) and bowling averages (45 wickets at 8.70) the same season, he was awarded a bat.

Alf Pope was also an all-rounder of note, a fast bowler, robust late-order batsman and a fine fielder. He made his first appearance for Derbyshire in 1930 and was a member of the Championship winning team of 1936. However he did not play for Chesterfield Cricket Club.

Eric and Harold both had a long involvement with the club. Harold, a leg-break bowler and lower-order batsman, played for the county in 1939 and 1946. In later years he captained Chesterfield's First Team. Eric was a playing member until he retired when he was 64. He captained the Second Eleven,

11. The cricketing Popes in 1952, Alf, Eric, Harold, George and Tony. (Tony Pope)

winning Bassetlaw 2A in 1968. Eric's son John joined him in the Second Eleven, the third generation of the Pope family to play for Chesterfield.

The 1930s were the golden years for Derbyshire, who were third in the County Championship in 1934, second in 1935 and winners in 1936. Of the winning eleven, six played for England at some stage of their career, Harry Elliott, Leslie Townsend, Bill Copson, Denis Smith, Stan Worthington and Tommy Mitchell. Three others played in almost every game, Alf Pope, Arthur Richardson (captain) and Albert Alderman. George Pope was missing for most of the season because of injury. The most remarkable game of the season at Chesterfield was against Northants when A.H. Bakewell carried his bat for 241 not out in the second innings to deny Derbyshire. Northamptonshire declared on 411 for 6 with Alf Pope taking all six wickets for 129 (10 for 187 in the match). Mitchell was unable to bowl in the second innings because of a broken finger; fortunately it was almost the end of the season. Sadly on the way home from the match there was a car accident in which Bakewell broke his arm so badly that he never played Championship cricket again. R.P. Northway, his opening partner, was killed.

During the Second World War there was a big military presence in and around the town and men in reserved occupations were less likely to be conscripted than during the First World War. The Park Annexe was requisitioned by the military for a drill ground and later for accommodation. The activities of Chesterfield Cricket Club were severely curtailed.

Chesterfield Cricket Club shared their ground with Chesterfield

Tube Works during the war, the Tube Works ground being out of commission, and also at some time during this period the Royal Engineers, who were stationed at the Boythorpe Drill Hall, played there. There were celebrity matches played between G.H. Pope's XI v the Mayor's XI when famous international players appeared (Colin Wilbourne)

The present scorebox was donated by Alderman Eastwood at the time of the alterations to the pavilion. It was constructed by the Derbyshire all-rounder Leslie Townsend, who was a time-served joiner.

My brother says that prior to the scoreboard gifted to the Park by Alderman Eastwood it was a wooden board painted green. Plates were hung on the hooks by young lads etc. Something else I did towards the end of the war was to score in the score box. The score box was presented to the Park by Alderman G.A. Eastwood. It was on wheels, but it never moved from its position just to the right of the pavilion adjacent to Park Road.[1] Anyway a pal of mine, Fred Ashby, said that they wanted lads to work the score box one Saturday. So we duly presented ourselves. It was a test to get it right, but we eventually perfected it. It took four lads to run it. I did the running total; two lads did the batsmen and one lad the fall of the last wicket and the two bowlers. We also had to liaise with the scorers downstairs, to keep things right. We had a free tea afterwards. Then we would go upstairs to meet the secretary in the left-hand side of the pavilion to see if he was satisfied with our performance and if we could come back next week and draw our wages. The wages depended on the collection round the ground. In my mind's eye, I think we got about 2s. 6d. which helped me to buy my first cycle. We were always requested to come back next week or on Bank Holiday, so we must have got things right. (Ken Silcock)

[1] It was moved a few yards further from the pavilion, presumably when the east terracing was built or soon afterwards.

3 Derbyshire County Cricket Club in Queen's Park, 1946–98

The Second World War brought Championship cricket to a halt. Derbyshire County Cricket Club played two one-day games at Chesterfield in 1945, before the Championship resumed a year later.

During the Second World War ground maintenance was carried out by the members of Chesterfield Cricket Club led by Sam Cantrill; inevitably the pitch could not be maintained to its previous high standard. Once more Queen's Park went into the history books when, after two overs, the pitch for the match against Yorkshire was found to be two yards too long and the match had to be restarted. Opinion was divided as to who was responsible. As the *Derbyshire Times* of 5 July 1946 reported:

> The preparation of the wicket in the first instance seems to be the responsibility of the Chesterfield Cricket Club and the marking for a county match is supervised by the Derbyshire groundsman Mr Walter Goodyear. Mr Goodyear told the press that he had some very willing helpers, but unknown to him one of them moved his guiding peg. The topic of how Derbyshire came to bat for two overs on a wicket 24 yards long will be discussed as long as cricket is played.

The journalist was right. Over 40 years later the Cricket Diary in the *Daily Telegraph* of 2 August 1990 recalled the episode in greater detail:

> Captain Pat Vaulkhard recalled that Frank Smailes bowled the first over to Denis Smith who struck two horrendous longhops for four apiece. Sir Len Hutton remembered that Bill Bowes bowled a maiden over. 'Bill was a better bowler than Smailes; he could cope with any length of pitch, but I came up from third man and told the captain that there was something wrong'. Brian Sellers, the Yorkshire captain, decided to bring out the chain and the pitch was found to be two yards too long. Captain Vaulkhard added 'The nine runs scored were scrubbed, the players left the field. The match started at ten minutes to 12, twenty minutes late. We had to play until ten minutes to seven.' Who was to blame? Mr Dean, who

had been a playing member and committee member of Chesterfield Cricket Club at the time, explained: 'At that time Chesterfield Cricket Club rented Queen's Park from the Corporation. We provided a groundsman, who worked with a ground committee, and he prepared county pitches which had to be approved by the county's groundsman, Mr Walter Goodyear. Mr Goodyear came to the ground some days before the Yorkshire match and marked the place he wished for the pitch by sticking a stump in the ground. The pitch was measured, but Mr Goodyear's mark was mistaken for a measured mark, so the pitch was too long.

One national paper commented: 'The normal length of a cricket pitch is 22 yards except at Chesterfield where they play to their own rules'. (Ken Silcock)

I had been playing cricket in Sheffield in the morning and cycled to the match arriving late. The Derbyshire score was negligible and when I asked what had happened, thinking that there might have been some rain, I was told that they had started late and why. The Chesterfield ground staff were insistent that it was not their fault and blamed the people from Derby. (John Redhead)

The other highlight of the season was the visit of the Indian tourists, who were very impressed by the carpet-bedding scheme in the form of the Indian badge. The match ended amidst great excitement as Harold Pope was bowled by Armanath with the second ball of the last possible over.

In October 1946, the Parks, Allotments & Cemeteries Committee of the Corporation resolved that the arrangements which had been made with Chesterfield Cricket Club should not be renewed and that in future the Corporation would be directly responsible for the maintenance of the pitch. They further resolved to make provision for its reconditioning. It was decided to purchase sight screens, practice nets, cricket tackle, scoreboards and ground cover etc. for £250 and a motor mower and other machines for £190. Shortly afterwards it was reported that equipment had been purchased from the Cricket Club for £50. No doubt with such savings it was felt that they could afford a clock on the outside of the pavilion as requested by Derbyshire. It was soon in need of repair.

Denis Smith, the very stylish left-hand opener, was a delight to watch. He could clip the ball off his toes like a male dancer. On one occasion he was batting at the Town Hall end when he hit a six which hit the clock on the pavilion and stopped it. What a sensation. It was several months before a repair was effected.

Derbyshire County Cricket Club and Chesterfield Borough Council were always short of money. It wasn't until the following year that normal service was resumed. (Ken Silcock)

Chesterfield Cricket Club were charged £40 for use of the ground, other local clubs £15. There were also charges laid down for the hire of equipment:

Hire of bats 2s. per bat per match or two hours net practice
Hire of balls 1s. per ball per match or two hours net practice
Hire of pads 2s. 6d. per set of three pairs per match or 10d. per two
    hours net practice
Gloves 2s. 6d. per three pairs (two pairs batsmen's and one pair
    wicket-keeper's) per match or 10d. per pair per two hours net
    practice

From 1947 the County Club dealt directly with the Corporation. To accommodate the large post-war crowds, temporary seating was installed on the cycle track around the cricket ground. In the years of austerity, Derbyshire paid 10 per cent gate receipts with a guaranteed minimum payment, £150 per season in 1947, rising to £250 in 1957. They also paid for gatemen and police, if required, and the hire of chairs at 3d. per day per chair, £25 for car parking and £1 5s. per match for the use of the turnstiles. They also contributed to the cost of terracing and a press box between the pavilion and the scoreboard and improvements to the pavilion, which included the extension of the balcony right across the front of the pavilion.

In 1947 Somerset were beaten in one day with G.H. Pope prominent with bat and ball. (Colin Wilbourne)

George Pope took 13 wickets for 50, conceding 24 runs before he took his first wicket.

I remember Derbyshire v Somerset in 1947; Derbyshire won by an innings in one day, the scores being Somerset 68 and 38, Derbyshire 231. The next match against Essex was remarkable for a last-wicket stand by Essex when number 11, Peter Smith, scored 163. I should imagine that after that Derbyshire lost. I also remember in that match a young Trevor Bailey standing under a steepling-high catch going into a spin and eventually not laying a hand on the ball. (David Short)

One of my most enjoyable memories of the Park was my first county cricket match on a June Saturday in 1948. Derbyshire v

Yorkshire was the game, and what a day's cricket we had. My pals and I arrived at the Park Road entrance to find things very busy, in fact we missed the toss and the first two wickets to go down, the queues were so long, the gate turned out to be 14,000, a ground record. George Pope was unplayable that day. After the match, so Derbyshire folklore tells us, George told Norman Yardley, Yorkshire and England captain at the time, to put that in his pipe and smoke it! George's swipe, so we are told, was due to the fact that he had been called into the England squad for the Test Match at Trent Bridge but was then made 12th man. George took umbrage at this and returned to play for his county, saying there was more to his talents than being a waiter, a reference to taking the drinks out. (Michael Cole)

Amazingly the captains agreed to the boundary line being reduced at lunchtime on the opening day to accommodate the large crowd.

Yorkshire won the toss and decided to bat. Herbert Halliday and Ted Lester opened the batting and Halliday took first strike. He wasn't satisfied with the position of the sight-screen at the lake end. It had to be moved and also the spectators, hell to play. Still not satisfied, more hell to play. All this time the late, great George Pope had the new ball in his hand, passing it one to the other, waiting patiently. Eventually Halliday was satisfied. The umpire called: 'Play' and the first ball from George shattered Halliday's stumps all over the place. The ground erupted. By lunch Yorkshire were all out for 44, including the captain Brian Sellers. Derbyshire went in after lunch and scored 277. So Yorkshire had to go in for 45 minutes and bang George did it again and by stumps Yorkshire were 19 for three. A great victory was in sight on Monday, but what happened? It rained all day. Tuesday wasn't much better. Yorkshire wouldn't come out to play. Spectators threw cushions at the Yorkshire dressing-room. Play eventually resumed, and at 6.30 p.m. Yorkshire were 37 for six and the match was drawn. What a dream it would have been if Derbyshire could have beaten a team of England players.[2]

Also in 1948 Derbyshire entertained Gloucestershire. On the final day they set Derbyshire 278 to win. Derbyshire kept losing wickets and it looked as though they would be defeated. George Pope came in at about number five and really set about the Gloucestershire bowling. The Derbyshire captain Gothard came in at number

---

[2] Although the Yorkshire team was without Hutton, Yardley and Coxon for this match, Derbyshire were without Townsend, Vaulkhard and Copson.

ten, batting with a runner, with Derbyshire requiring 81 to win and only two wickets left. Would Derbyshire be bowled out or would they win? The runs mounted and Gothard managed to keep the ball out. George Pope played a terrific innings of 125 not out and Derbyshire won the match with a few minutes to spare. What a marvellous pair of players on the day. Whilst George was playing this fantastic knock, he hit a six from the pavilion end, which landed on the first island in the lake; they had to get a rowing boat to retrieve the ball, what a hit!

But the greatest hit I ever saw still takes a bit of believing. The Derbyshire captain at the time was Pat Vaulkhard. He was a farmer and couldn't half hit a cricket ball. I can't remember the opposition, but I was sitting on the grass adjacent to the bandstand area. Pat was batting at the pavilion end, when he pulled a ball over square leg. It was a queer sensation as the ball passed over our heads whistling like an express train. The ball landed on the asphalt and shattered and they had to finish the over with another ball. What a moment, did it happen or did we dream it up? Something I shall never forget. (Ken Silcock)

George Pope completed the double of 1,000 runs and 100 wickets in all first-class matches in 1938 and in 1948 he completed the double for Derbyshire matches during the match against Surrey at Chesterfield. It was his final game for the county as he missed the last few matches of the season because of a strained back. Despite finishing the top of the Derbyshire batting averages and second in the bowling averages he decided to retire at the age of 37.

George became a first-class umpire after retiring. Later on in life, I knew him quite well via the top bar of the King and Miller. George was so well known and respected, I never saw him buy himself a drink. He always had a half of bitter. He would be treated to possibly two halves and then he always had to go to 'another meeting' and would disappear to another pub to be treated like Royalty. (Ken Silcock)

My first match for Derbyshire was at Queen's Park in 1949. It was against Kent and we didn't do very well. When I went in to bat, the score was 16 for five wickets. I was out first ball, caught behind by Godfrey Evans. The second innings was better as I made 22 and I took three catches so it wasn't all bad! (George Lowe)

There was another heavy defeat a few weeks later when Gloucestershire won by ten wickets with J.K.R. Graveney taking all ten wickets in the second innings.

SCORE CARD, PRICE 3d.   TOSS WON BY KENT.
This card does not necessarily include fall of the last wicket.

Queen's Park, Chesterfield.   June 22nd, 23rd and 24th.

DERBYSHIRE v. KENT

Hours of Play—
First Day–11.30 to 7.   Second Day–11.30 to 7.   Third Day–11 to 4 or 4.30

Lunch—1.30 to 2.10

KENT	First Innings.		Second Innings.	
1 Todd L J	lbw b Jackson	50	b Gladwin	19
2 Mayes R	ct Lowe b Copson	2	lbw b Gladwin	4
3 Ames L E G	b Gladwin	4	lbw b Jackson	58
4 Hearn P	ct Copson b Rhodes	26	ct Dawkes b Jackson	3
5 Phebey A H	b Jackson	68	b Rhodes	1
6 Evans T G	ct Revill b Jackson	24	ct Townsend b Jackson	15
7 Edrich B R	ct Lowe b Gladwin	37	ct Revill b Gladwin	46
8 D G Clark	ct Revill b Rhodes	14	b Gladwin	14
9 Dovey R R	not out	31	ct Skinner b Gladwin	6
10 Ridgway F	ct Marsh b Rhodes	0	ct Lowe b Rhodes	10
11 Lewis C	b Jackson	0	not out	0
	Extras— b-6 lb-3 w- nb-	9	b-5 lb-4 w- nb-1	10
	Total	265	Total	166

Umpires—
A. R. Coleman & H. Elliott

Fall of Wickets.—1st Inns.
1   2   3   4   5   6   7   8   9   10   1   2   3   4   5   6   7   8   9   10
3 18 79 99 137 199 224 264 265 265   6 40 56 57 78 94 146 156 166 166

Bowling Analysis :	O	M	R	W	O	M	R	W
Copson W	11	4	16	1	13	3	35	0
Gladwin C	19	4	57	2	15	3	41	5
Jackson L	33.1	10	63	4	13	2	36	3
Rhodes A E	34	15	114	3	15.1	3	44	2
Marsh E	2	0	6	0				

DERBYSHIRE	First Innings.		Second Innings.	
1 Elliott C S	run out	6	ct Ridgway b Lewis	59
2 Townsend A	ct Todd b Ridgway	0	b Ridgway	0
3 Revill A	b Dovey	7	b Dovey	0
4 Marsh E	lbw b Ridgway	0	ct Ames b Dovey	24
5 Gladwin C	run out	0	b Ridgway	3
6 D A Skinner	ct Evans b Dovey	0	ct Edrich b Ridgway	0
7 G Lowe	ct Evans b Ridgway	0	b Dovey	22
8 Dawkes G	lbw b Dovey	8	lbw b Edrich	38
9 Rhodes A E	ct Edrich b Ridgway	36	ct Evans b Lewis	10
10 Copson W	ct Phebey b Dovey	0	not out	5
11 Jackson L	not out	1	b Lewis	2
	Extras— b-2 lb-2 w- nb-	4	b-2 lb-8 w-1 nb-	11
	Total	82	Total	233

‡ captain.   * wicket-keeper.
Scorers—C. Baker & E. Hoskins.

Fall of Wickets.—1st Inns.
1   2   3   4   5   6   7   8   9   10   1   2   3   4   5   6   7   8   9   10
3 15 16 16 19 36 64 76 82   5 118 124 134 138 194 211 226 226 233

Bowling Analysis :	O	M	R	W	O	M	R	W
Ridgway F	11.4	1	43	4	27	9	37	3
Todd L J	4	2	4	0	6	3	6	0
Dovey R R	11	5	19	4	28	10	62	3
Lewis C	4	0	12	0	23.1	10	44	3
Edrich B R					19	4	73	1

MAKES THE BEST SHANDY

12. The familiar buff-coloured scorecard for George Lowe's debut. Cliff Gladwin batted at number five and his fellow fast bowlers were Copson and Jackson. (George Lowe)

In 1950 the West Indians came to town, the famous 'W's , Everton Weekes, Clyde Walcott and Frank Worrell. Park full, match of the year for Derbyshire who relied heavily on a good tourist match, good weather etc. to boost the financial coffers. Anyway the West Indians won the toss and elected to bat. They had forgotten about Cliff Gladwin and Les Jackson, two of the finest county seam bowlers in the country at the time. Bang, in about half an hour the West Indians were 23 for four. Alarm bells rang in the Derbyshire Secretary's office, above the dressing room on the left-hand side of the pavilion. Frantic signals from the pavilion: 'Get them off' so two spinners had to come on. Frantic cries from the loyal supporters, but no use, money came first, so the West Indians made a presentable total. In the end it didn't matter because it rained over the weekend so the match was rain affected and it finished up as a draw. So again, what could have been a great victory just fizzled out. (Ken Silcock)

Then it was the turn of the Indian tourists.

One Tuesday night in July 1952 my pal came over and said: 'The Indians are in Queen's Park tomorrow, do you fancy going?' I was 14 at the time and it was just before the summer holidays. So, after telling my mother we would not be missing anything at school, we set off the following morning with sandwiches packed and a bottle of pop. When we got on the bus at Stonebroom we noticed that two or three more lads were on the bus and by the time we arrived at the ground half the class, including most of the school cricket team, were there. We saw a great day's play. Derbyshire bowled out the tourists for 86 (Les Jackson six for 39 and Derek Morgan three for 35).The next morning the order came: 'Would those lads who spent yesterday at Queen's Park report to the headmaster's study.' We all received the cane, but it had been worth the punishment to see Les, the first of many great performances in the Park. (Ray Farnsworth)

Needing 373 to win, India were 115 for three when rain stopped play and the match was drawn.
   The Australians were the tourists in 1953.

I took five for 36 in the second innings as they were dismissed for 146. This was the performance of the week according to the *Sporting Record* and the prize was a Ronson cigarette lighter with my name engraved on it. Unfortunately I lost it in the Odeon cinema. I was also given a scorecard with lettering in gold. (Edwin Smith)

Edwin Smith had made his debut for Derbyshire two seasons earlier, when just 17-years-old. In his second match, against Worcestershire at Chesterfield, he took eight of the last nine wickets to fall for 21 runs in 10.2 overs.
   There were some close finishes.

Lancashire were beaten by 49 runs with five minutes remaining for play in 1953 and three years later Yorkshire were beaten by six runs, when Harold Rhodes bowled them to victory. (Colin Wilbourne)

13. Derbyshire v Yorkshire 1956. Laurie Johnson, Alan Revill, Donald Carr and Derek Morgan look on as George Dawkes takes a catch off the bowling of Cliff Gladwin. (*Sheffield Telegraph and Star*)

My earliest recollection is the match against Yorkshire in 1956. I was on leave from National Service and we beat the Tykes by six runs in a most thrilling match. (Harold Rhodes)

Of all my memories of cricket in the Park (particularly from the 1950s and 1960s when Derbyshire had a team that could compete with the best) the annual encounter against the old enemy, Yorkshire, was the highlight of the season. As soon as the fixtures were published you would mark the date on the calendar. If the weather was fine you had to be there for the start of play to get your favourite seat on the old wooden benches on the terraces. Many's the time I queued with my father at the Park Road entrance waiting for the turnstiles to open. Very often the queue would stretch back over the level crossing, under the railway bridge and up to the corner opposite the Queen's Park Hotel. Then a coal train would appear on the branch line on its way to Robinsons' factories or the gas works and the crossing gates would be closed disrupting the queue and everyone grumbled. With the ground packed, by the afternoon it would be standing room only. The atmosphere was often electric with the only light relief coming from the good natured banter between the rival supporters. I witnessed many of the games in that era and, if I had to pick one out, it would be the match in 1957.

This match had been chosen by Les Jackson for his benefit match after ten years faithful service to Derbyshire. The 11,000 spectators who turned up on the Saturday saw John Kelly defy the Yorkshire attack, which included Trueman, Wardle and Illingworth, to score 106 out of a total of 292. Despite a century by Brian Close on the Monday, Gladwin and Jackson took eight wickets between them as Yorkshire were bowled out for 199. Some quick scoring by the captain, Donald Carr, and George Dawkes enabled Derbyshire to declare and set Yorkshire 325 runs to win. On that Tuesday afternoon Les Jackson proved what a great bowler he was by taking a further six wickets (11 for 114 in the match) and bowling Derbyshire to victory with just eight minutes to spare. It doesn't get any better than that. (Ray Farnsworth)

A month later the West Indians were the visitors.

My earliest memory of watching cricket in the Park was when I was taken as a very small boy by my father to see the visiting West Indian team. On a glorious Saturday afternoon of high summer we were part of a very large crowd and I recall that we sat on the bank

14. The packed crowd for the Derbyshire v West Indians match in 1957. (*Derbyshire Countryside*)

roughly opposite the scoreboard. I had heard that one of the players was a fearsome fast bowler by the name of Roy Gilchrist and I was therefore determined to keep a sharp lookout for him, probably pestering my father every few minutes or so to identify him for me on the field. Derbyshire were batting and at one point my father announced that they were proceeding at the rate of 55 runs per hour. This meant nothing to me and when I asked my Dad if that was good he replied with some feeling that it was absolutely awful — clearly a reflection of the standards expected by cricket supporters at that time. (John Cook)

I have rarely seen so many people packed into the ground as there were on the first day (Saturday). It was very hot and humid and by mid-afternoon the caterers had just about sold out, no pop, no ice-cream and the queue at the beer tent took half an hour to get served. In the morning Gladwin was virtually unplayable and the tourists collapsed to 115 all out, but Derbyshire didn't fare much better and at the close were 98 for five. The weather continued hot and sunny so I decided to take Monday off work (without pay) to go and see if Derbyshire could pull off a victory. It was not to be, but what a marvellously entertaining day the large crowd enjoyed. In the afternoon we were treated to a scintillating batting display from the young Collie Smith. He had been bowled first ball by Gladwin in the first innings, but he extracted full revenge that

15. Alf Valentine keeps his eye on the cricket as he signs autographs. (*Derbyshire Countryside*)

afternoon, hitting Gladwin on to the pavilion roof for one of the four sixes he struck in a brilliant innings of 133. I am sure that I was not alone amongst those present that afternoon in considering this innings one of the very best ever seen at Queen's Park. The West Indians won comfortably in the end. (Ray Farnsworth)

Collie Smith scored a brilliant 133 which was followed by a devastating spell of fast bowling by Roy Gilchrist. It was an electric atmosphere as he ran up to bowl in dead silence (a bit different from today's crowds). Arnold Hamer, Charlie Lee, Donald Carr and Alan Revill probably found it their most scary experience against a fast bowler. (David Short)

In July Middlesex were the opposition for an extraordinary match.

In the period between our arrival after school and the close of play my friends and I saw 12 wickets fall for 82 runs with 50 of those made in 40 minutes by George Dawkes and Derek Morgan, as Derbyshire scored 153 in reply to Middlesex's score of 102. When Middlesex started their second innings they lost their first wicket to the second ball of the innings, three more wickets taking the score to one for four, the fifth wicket fell at nine. Fred Titmus walked slowly to the wicket to waste time, but only lasted two balls. Donald Carr claimed the extra half-hour, but when the score reached 11 for six, it began to rain and play ended for the day. Unfortunately we were at school next morning when Middlesex lost three more wickets with the score at 13 before Bennett and Moss saved Middlesex from complete humiliation by adding 16 for the last wicket. What would have been the score if bad light and rain had not intervened? (Janet Murphy)

16. Didn't we do well! Les Jackson and Cliff Gladwin after the match against Middlesex. (Raymond's Photographic Agency)

The bowlers were not always on top.

> I remember Bill Edrich making 208 not out. He hit some huge sixes, the ball going way above my head as I fielded at long on. In a match against Gloucestershire, Tom Graveney scored 222, but I had him lbw for nought in the second! (Edwin Smith)

Cliff Gladwin's last match at Chesterfield in 1958 ended in spectacular fashion.

> Worcestershire wanted just 135 to win and they had clawed their way to 117 for nine when there was a terrific storm. The rain came down so hard that the groundsmen who had taken the covers out sheltered underneath them — the noise must have been deafening! Ten minutes later the pitch was flooded and the spectators had to paddle their way out of the ground. (Janet Murphy)

Derbyshire were gradually bowling Worcestershire out and it

looked odds on Cliff would finish on the winning side, but all the time, which was a credit to both sides, the match had been played in a slight drizzle. The last two batsmen were at the wicket, and Derbyshire's victory appeared imminent when bang, the heavens opened, and it did not stop to rain. The two groundsmen who pulled out the covers stayed under them as it was so awful. I was sheltering in the beer tent with my best friend Geoffrey Boden, when suddenly the water came through the canvas, flooding us out. Geoff and I were positively wet through. We dashed home to Boythorpe. Mother went ballistic, we were both due to catch the midnight train to Bournemouth on Friday night for a week's holiday. Anyway after having a hot bath, Mother managed to salvage some clothes and Geoff and I departed.

Mansfield Brewery ran the beer tent for many years. On another occasion business was brisk in the beer tent when suddenly a violent thunderstorm occurred. A terrific wind got up which caused the tent to collapse. Len Slater, who worked at the *Sheffield Telegraph and Star*, a printer on nights, always ran the bar during the cricket matches. The tent collapsed on him. He was very lucky, he was taken to the Royal Hospital and survived; others were shaken, but not seriously injured. (Ken Silcock)

When the great Surrey team of the 1950s made a rare visit to Chesterfield in 1958, I was revising for exams. The first day was washed out. Laker, Loader and Lock were playing for England, but the Test Match finished early and as the toss had not been made in the Championship match, they were added to the Surrey team. Eventually the temptation was too great and I went down to the Park to watch the last 15 minutes play, but Derbyshire had declared and Surrey were batting so I didn't get to see them bowl. At close of play, I turned round to go home and found my chemistry mistress standing behind me. Fortunately I didn't have a chemistry exam the next day! (Janet Murphy)

I remember walking out to bat against Somerset scoring about 19 in about 70 minutes. The next time I played for the County at Chesterfield was about three years later again going out to bat on a Saturday afternoon in front of a big crowd. This was against Warwickshire and was undoubtedly my finest hour as I was 77 not out at the close of play. Unfortunately I was unable to complete a hundred on the Monday morning, but Derbyshire won the match. I have never played in finer matches than in Queen's Park at the weekend. (David Short)

17. Neil Harvey and Donald Carr inspect the pitch before the Derbyshire v Australia match in 1961. Unfortunately the match was ruined by rain. (Chesterfield Borough Council)

Queen's Park is my favourite cricket ground in the country, excluding the Test Match venues and, even including them, comes a close second behind only the incomparable Lord's. I made my debut for Derbyshire in 1959 against Yorkshire in Queen's Park in front of a big crowd and have great memories of that match, which we sadly lost after our declaration in the second innings. (Ian Buxton)

For the spectators, matches against the touring sides were always keenly anticipated, but the weather was not always kind. In 1961 a large amount of extra seating was installed and facilities improved for spectators for the visit of the Australians. It rained and only 22 overs were bowled.

> Derbyshire supporters have never understood why Les Jackson was selected to play for England on only two occasions. The second time was in 1961. By coincidence Derbyshire were playing at Chesterfield at the same time. The batsmen were surprised when applause rang round the ground during a quiet period of play — Les Jackson had hit a four in the Test Match at Headingley. After it happened a second time the public address system asked the crowd not to applaud Jackson's exploits. (Janet Murphy)

Donald Carr played his last match as Derbyshire's captain at Chesterfield in 1962. Requiring five runs for his 1,000 for the season he faced the bowling of John Price who bowled a wide longhop outside the off stump. Carr stepped back to cut the ball and edged a catch to John Murray. The snick could be heard around the ground, but no one appealed and Carr went on to reach his 1,000 runs (Derbyshire only wanted 49 to win).

Derbyshire's first professional captain was Charlie Lee, who is remembered as a dour batsman, but he had a fund of amusing anecdotes, often against himself, as he related in the 1970 (Centenary Year) edition of the *Derbyshire County Cricket Year Book.*

> At Chesterfield against Sussex Laurie Johnson 'bagged a pair' and as he reached the edge of the ground two ducks from the lake walked off with him. Once more at Chesterfield, I was walking out

to bat with Laurie Johnson and I clearly heard the remark: 'There they go, the quick and the dead'.

When Donald Carr put me on to bowl against Glamorgan at Chesterfield a wag shouted: 'Nay, Donald, don't 'purrimon', if he bowls as fast as he bats he'll not gerrit to t'other bloody end'.

Donald Carr returned for four matches in August, scoring 136 against Sussex in his first innings since his retirement. In the same match Bob Taylor took six catches in Sussex's first innings, equalling the Derbyshire record for wicket-keepers: only two wickets fell in their second innings. A few weeks later he did even better as he took five catches in each innings of the match against Hampshire equalling the then record for the number of catches in a match by a Derbyshire wicket-keeper.

Geoff Boycott's three centuries against Derbyshire is the highest number by an opposing batsman at Chesterfield, but in 1964 there was a rare failure.

I remember bowling Boycott before he got double figures. (Brian Jackson)

When the South Africans visited England in 1965, there was a concern that the games might be interrupted by anti-apartheid demonstrators. Their match at Chesterfield hit the headlines for a different reason.

There was the infamous no-balling episode of the fast bowler Harold Rhodes in the match against the touring South Africans in

18. The South Africans pose by the carpet bedding. Eddie Barlow is fourth from the right. (Chesterfield Borough Council)

June 1965. Test umpire Sid Buller no-balled the Derbyshire player, top of the national bowling averages, for throwing, a policy many believed to have been initiated by the Lord's hierarchy. The packed crowd was incensed, barracking and slow-handclapping the umpire. Newspaper sellers added their cries, doing a brisk business as the incident made the late news section of the *Star* the same afternoon. Mr Buller had to have a police escort off the field, one irate member waving his stick at the umpire. Amidst international publicity, Derbyshire reacted in the only way they could, comprehensively defeating the tourists, with their stars such as Barlow, Pollock and Bland, by seven wickets. The throwing controversy robbed a fine player of further Test appearances and shortened his county career. (Roger Hartley)

The next morning there were almost as many press photographers on the ground as players. Next day my photograph was on the front page of the *Sun* — well I knew it was me! (Janet Murphy)

I remember the match vividly; I think Harold was unfairly treated. My own personal highlight was bowling Graeme Pollock. We were given a bottle of South African sherry for winning. (Brian Jackson)

19. Members of the local constabulary enjoy the sunshine as Laurie Johnson leaves the field at the end of the game. Sid Buller is in the midst of the South Africans. (Janet Murphy)

A strong, but not happy, memory was the calling of Harold Rhodes for throwing by Sid Buller in the win over the South Africans. There are many more happy memories of my playing days in Queen's Park and I am really pleased that there is first-class cricket being played again on this beautiful ground. (Ian Buxton)

Queen's Park has always been my favourite cricket ground. Some people may find that strange as it was at Queen's Park that an incident occurred which put an end to my Test career. The match was soured by Sid Buller's actions, although Derbyshire went on to record a famous victory beating the South Africans by seven wickets. In fact Derbyshire were the only side to beat the tourists — South Africa beat England 1 – 0 in the Test series.[1] (Harold Rhodes)

Brian Jackson and Harold Rhodes topped the national bowling averages for that season. Opening the batting for the South Africans was Eddie Barlow, later to become a very popular Derbyshire captain.

By the 1960s the closure of the Park for cricket matches increasingly upset those not interested in the game.

In the playground there was a brick entrance containing two iron turnstiles from Boythorpe Road. The Queen's Park was closed for the six county cricket matches played on the cricket field, so for 18 days each year notices were posted on each of the three entrances each time to that effect. It caused a bit of resentment and grumbling, but people had to walk round on these occasions. A kindly doorkeeper would let through a mother with a pram or pushchair or possibly a 'babe in arms', but it did not cause too much upset. But later the general public said that it was their Park and why should it be closed for these long periods. So the rules were relaxed and fencing put along the side of the ground adjacent to the bandstand. But it was a laugh really because by this time the bridge had been placed over Markham Road and the general public could see without paying. The only advantage for those who paid was that they could obtain a seat in the pavilion area or the bench seats situated round the ground on the cycle track. (Ken Silcock)

At one point my friend and I got bored and went to the playground which I believe was situated near the swimming baths at the time. When we wanted to return to watch the cricket, the gateman would not let us back in — our tickets were with my

---

[1] They were also defeated by T.N. Pearce's XI at the Scarborough Festival.

friend's father. Luckily my friend and I managed to get past a different gateman who was manning the Boythorpe Avenue entrance and return to the match. (Steve Franks)

The 1960s brought changes with the introduction of one-day games and Sunday play. On 21 May 1966 Derbyshire played their first home Gillette Cup match at Chesterfield which Essex won by two wickets. The same year the International Cavaliers were due to play a televised match for Edwin Smith's testimonial, but rain prevented any play. Chesterfield Borough Council would not allow the Park to be closed for Sunday play so fencing was erected along the bank and admission charged for entry to the enclosure for the first Sunday play in the Championship, which took place on 20 May 1967, when Surrey were the visitors. The 32 overs bowled were the only ones bowled in the match due to rain, but on a Sunday in August over 2,000 spectators watched Derbyshire v Warwickshire.

> We were playing Yorkshire. I had made just two when Brian Close dropped me at second slip off the bowling of Fred Trueman. By the afternoon I had made about 70 when Close asked Trueman to bowl again, but Fred refused. 'Bugger off', he said, 'Yon Oxford muppet should've been in t'hutch first thing this morning'. So Nicholson was brought on to bowl instead. Close then posted all of his fielders on the off side with the exception of Fred who was left to cover the leg side and we were able to score easy runs to leg. A breathless Fred was more than happy to come back and bowl the next over! (Peter Gibbs)

The Australians were back in 1968.

> The match against the Australians was a good one. The weather was fine, there was a big crowd, the pitch was good and the cricket was of a high standard with the Australians winning by just eight runs. (Peter Gibbs)

> I was batting with Edwin Smith and we added 17 runs for the last wicket (I got one) before Edwin edged one to slip when on 31. Neil Hawke breathed a sigh of relief. (Brian Jackson)

Harold Rhodes was the beneficiary in 1968. A match against the International Cavaliers was televised from the Park at the beginning of September. Unfortunately rain brought proceedings to an end after just 65 minutes play but there was time for spectators to see 47-year-old Les Jackson bowl nine overs taking two for 19, including the prize scalp of Geoff Boycott. The brightest innings came from a young Barry Richards.

20. A dismal sight as the crowd wait for the match against the International Cavaliers to begin. (Pat Pick)

21. Frank Bough interviews Geoffrey Boycott. (Pat Pick)

22. Harold Rhodes takes the field in his benefit match, flanked by Ian Redpath and John Inverarity of Australia. (Pat Pick)

The first John Player League match at Chesterfield was on 29 June 1969, but it was the Gillette Cup match a few weeks later that was the more memorable.

The most exciting one-day match ever seen at Queen's Park was Derbyshire's victory over Sussex on 30 July 1969, a semi-final of the Gillette Cup. 10,582 spectators watched a famous victory over the masters of one-day cricket at that time. The day was fine, but the pitch damp, and Derbyshire struggled to what appeared to be a weak total of 136, sections of the crowd shouting their disapproval. However the Sussex innings began in a hushed atmosphere more like that of a match at the Crucible, as our two friends, Rhodes and Ward, steamed in. After 14 tense overs the usually flamboyant Martlets had scored only ten runs for two wickets. The roar at the end of each maiden over was deafening. The rotund, popular Fred Rumsey and the Hathersage-born Peter Eyre continued the fiery onslaught, man of the match Peter picking up six wickets as the Sussex men were humbled for just 49 runs. Hundreds inspected the straw-coloured pitch after the match and dwelled to savour the moment, though not with amber nectar as the beer tents had run dry early in the Sussex innings! We journeyed to the final at Lord's, where Derbyshire lost a disappointing match to Yorkshire, but the memory of the semi-final victory matures like old port. (Roger Hartley)

23. Somewhere in there is a cricket pitch – the massed crowd at the end of the Gillette Cup semi-final. (Souvenir Brochure Gillette Cup Final)

It was a strange match, the pitch was very wet and it was difficult to know what would be an adequate total. We thought that 136 was a reasonable score, but the crowd made it plain that they didn't think it was enough. It was a very exciting game played in front of a packed crowd. The presentation at the end for Man of the Match was on the outfield and we were surrounded by the crowd – that probably wouldn't be allowed today. (Peter Gibbs)

In my last season, 1969, there was another famous victory against Sussex in the Gillette Cup semi-final in front of one of the biggest crowds I saw at the Park. (Harold Rhodes)

Having lived in Sussex I didn't know who to support. Fortunately I chose Derbyshire. (John Bolton)

Somerset were the visitors in a Championship match the same season.

We were playing Somerset and I was on 99. Their slow bowler Robinson was running up to bowl when something distracted him. He tried to stop the ball, but let it go and it trickled down the wicket. I walked down the wicket and clipped the ball for four sweet as a nut to reach my century. Somerset were not happy saying I had taken advantage of the situation, but it was something that I was perfectly entitled to do. (Peter Gibbs)

The happiest day for me at Queen's Park was undoubtedly Sunday 3 May 1970. It was my first year as captain and the second John Player League match of the season was at Chesterfield against Yorkshire on this day. I had played against them every year since 1959 and never been on the winning side — until this special day. Yes, it was a Sunday League match, but it was victory and a comfortable one too in front another large crowd and I can still feel the thrill and satisfaction of this first win after so many years of only painful near misses and failure against them. (Ian Buxton)

In July a large crowd gathered to watch old favourites such as George Dawkes, Cliff Gladwin and Les Jackson in a one-day match as Derbyshire defeated the MCC (including nine Derbyshire veterans) by 58 runs in a match to celebrate the centenary of the founding of Derbyshire County Cricket Club.

Chris Wilkins made the joint fastest hundred of the season against Worcestershire to win a Ford Capri car. (Phil Russell)

24. The Derbyshire team in the centenary year. *Left to right:* Fred Swarbrook, Peter Gibbs, Alan Ward, Mike Hendrick, Edwin Smith, Ian Buxton, John Harvey, Chris Wilkins, Bob Taylor, David Smith and Ian Hall. (Chesterfield Borough Council)

His 102 (five sixes and seven fours) took 70 minutes and with Peter Gibbs he added 47 runs in 18 minutes.

During the year the Council held discussions with Derbyshire County Cricket Club who wanted to use an area of land in Queen's Park for erection of a sports club and centre together with adaptations to the pavilion. The scheme was agreed to in principle, but the club had difficulty in raising funds and the scheme was not carried through.

In 1971 slow bowler Fred Swarbrook took an unexpected wicket in the Championship match against Yorkshire.

> Mike Hendrick had bowled really well without success, then Fred Swarbrook bowled a longhop to Boycott who hit it straight into the hands of the fielder at cover. Everyone fell about laughing except Boycott. (Janet Murphy)

Chris Wilkins is best remembered as an attacking batsman and an outstanding fielder, but against the Pakistanis in 1972 it was his bowling that was memorable.

> Chris got a wicket bowling right-arm over in the first innings and left-arm round in the second. (Phil Russell)

Zaheer Abbas was the batsman on both occasions, and he was not amused. Two years later the atmosphere was rather different.

> There was an almost unique occasion on a cricket pitch (in fact the third time in nearly two centuries of first-class cricket) when a player was sent off the pitch, not by an umpire, but by his own captain. The offending player was the Dronfield-born Alan Ward who had showed such promise in his early career for county and country. In a match in the Park in June 1973, against Yorkshire, Alan picked up Boycott's wicket, but then struggled to find his rhythm and bowled numerous no-balls for overstepping the bowling crease. Called back for a second spell by the captain Brian Bolus, he maintained that he had lost his confidence, but Bolus was not for arguing and gestured for all the crowd to see for Ward to leave. The bowler did not appear again that season and only fitfully after that, another career foreshortened. (Roger Hartley)

> Playing for Derbyshire I was lucky enough to play on most of the famous cricket grounds in England i.e. all the 'Test Match' venues plus lovely grounds such as the universities of Oxford (The Parks) and Cambridge (Fenner's) and the Duchess of Norfolk's ground at Arundel. However I always regarded Queen's Park as my favourite ground and made my highest scores for Derbyshire there (141 not out against Warwickshire was my highest first-class score and 76 not out against Middlesex, my highest one-day score). The pitch at Queen's Park just seemed to suit me as it usually had plenty of pace and bounce and helped me play shots. Another game I remember quite clearly was against the Australian tourists in the mid 70s on another particularly fast, bouncy pitch. Len Pascoe, the Aussies' opening bowler was really firing them down and I decided that anything pitched 'in my half' was going to get the full treatment. I've never seen so many 'slips' in place as I kept throwing the bat at anything pitched up. I'm sure there must have been six or seven fielders in the 'slip cordon' plus a fly slip stationed half-way to the boundary. I still managed to nick a few through before getting out to their leg-spinner. The Aussie fielders, of course, weren't shy at making a few comments as I kept on playing and missing! (Harry Cartwright)

Once more the County Club was in financial trouble and the tenancy of the playing area at Derby was given up from 5 May 1975 although the office space was retained. Chesterfield was now Derbyshire's principal ground with 19 days cricket in 1975 and 20 days the following year. Consideration was again given to moving the headquarters to Chesterfield and a new development was proposed comprising squash courts, indoor cricket nets and social facilities in a new pavilion with a 99-year lease to enable the club to raise the necessary finance. In view of the type of lease required and the loss of the tennis courts in Queen's Park Annexe to make way for car parking the Recreation and Leisure Committee recommended that the scheme should be turned down.

Leicestershire won their first County Championship title when they defeated Derbyshire in the last match of the season in September 1975. As the bonus points gained were sufficient to give them the Championship Chris Balderstone was allowed to dash north to play in a Football League match at Doncaster on the evening of the second day. He completed a century next morning and took three for 28 in the afternoon as Leicestershire duly won the match.

The following year was notable for the arrival of Eddie Barlow. He made an early impact at Chesterfield, scoring 69 as Derbyshire beat Glamorgan in the Benson and Hedges Cup by eight wickets with five overs to spare, and the next day scoring 77 (five fours and four sixes) as Derbyshire beat Lancashire by five runs in a John Player League game.

In 1977 Colin Tunnicliffe and Fred Swarbrook scored 17 off the last over to beat Surrey by one wicket in a John Player League game, Tunnicliffe finishing the match with a six off the last ball.

It was the fielding exploits of Phil Russell which caused the headlines in 1978. In May he took five catches in the first innings of the match against the Pakistanis. It was the third time a Derbyshire player had taken five catches in an innings and each time it had been at Chesterfield; the others were Charlie Lee against Lancashire and Derek Morgan against Glamorgan, both in 1960. The wearing of a helmet was still comparatively unusual in 1978. Fortunately Russell was wearing one during the Derbyshire v Glamorgan match a few weeks later.

We were due to take the new ball and, as Harry Cartwright had a bad back, I volunteered for the 'bat-pad' position. This was the first time I had worn a helmet in this position so I thought I would be safe if hit on the head. Colin Tunnicliffe took the new ball from the lake end bowling (uphill) to Malcolm Nash, a left-hander. He picked the delivery up off his legs and normally I would have turned away on seeing the stroke, but as I was wearing the helmet, I stayed down. The ball went through the grid and settled between the wire and my right cheek-bone, breaking it. My reaction was to pull the ball out upon which the captain Eddie Barlow appealed for a catch. The umpire Dickie Bird called: 'Dead ball' and Arthur Jepson at square leg called: 'Dead man you mean'. Dickie immediately ran off and rang Lord's for clarification while I was helped from the field. From that day the law was implemented that the batsman could not be given out caught if the ball came off a fielder's helmet. (Phil Russell)

Soon afterwards Glamorgan folded to an innings defeat. Russell was fortunate to escape with no more than a fractured-cheek bone, a chipped tooth and deep facial bruising. Returning from hospital he commented: 'I have probably got off quite well' — something of an understatement.

Throughout the 1970s the pitches had a very high reputation. Harold Graham, who had been appointed in 1953, won Groundsman of the Year awards for the grounds on which a limited number of games were played in 1974 and 1978: the second time posthumously following his death at the early age of 56. Harold was followed by his son Norman until he became grounds-man at Essex.

In 1980 John Wright scored 96 against Andy Roberts, Joel Garner and Malcolm Marshall on a green pitch. Hendrick dismissed the same three bowlers for a hat-trick. The West Indians required eight to win so Wright bowled the second over and had Bacchus caught off a longhop with his first ball in first-class cricket.

> David Steele said that it was the best innings he had ever seen.
> (David Griffin)

There was a remarkable finish in a John Player League game against Essex the same season.

> Derbyshire batted first and scored 148. Because of rain Essex had a reduced target of 110 in 29 overs. At 98 for four, and with the two batsmen, Fletcher and Pont, having put on 70, Essex needed only 12 more runs with seven overs to go and six wickets left and seemed to be well on their way to victory. Fletcher was dismissed for 56 and the wickets fell regularly until the last over began when Essex, with one wicket left, required three runs to win. They were all out for 107 leaving Derbyshire the winners by two runs with two balls left. The unlikely hero was David Steele, with three wickets for ten runs, nine of which came from his first over. (Janet Murphy)

Cricket returned to Derby in 1977, but there was still uncertainty as to where the headquarters should be. In 1980 the Council and the County Club failed to agree over the number of days cricket to be played at Chesterfield the following season. When the fixture list was published for 1981 all home matches were scheduled for Derby, a decision confirmed by the Derbyshire

The visit of the Indians in 1959 coincided with a long, hot summer. (Mrs Rogers)

The West Indian side for this match included Rohan Kanhai, Gary Sobers, Wes Hall, Charlie Griffith and Lance Gibbs. (Mrs Rogers)

The Australians won the match by the narrow margin of eight runs. (Mrs Rogers)

Fran O'Neill presents the commemorative glassware to Jim
Brailsford, both are wearing their Derbyshire Gentlemen's
blazers. (Jim Brailsford)

Committee in November. Possibly they had underestimated the strength of feeling in the north of the county. Leading the protests against the decision was the Chesterfield Cricket Lovers' Society. The society had been founded in 1963 by Frank Gordon Robinson when he sent a letter to the *Derbyshire Times* inviting other cricket lovers in the area to contact him with the view to forming a society in which lovers of the game could get together from time to time. The society is still thriving. A special meeting was held at Derby to debate the resolution: 'That 19 days county cricket be continued at Queen's Park, Chesterfield in 1981 and subsequent seasons.' No doubt the County Committee was relieved when the motion was defeated with voting 861 to 753 in the club's favour. However 11 days cricket were reinstated for 1981 and 15 days the following season.

In August 1981 another scheme was proposed for a headquarters at Chesterfield, but the following year the foundation stone for a new pavilion at Derby was laid and any possibility of moving the headquarters to Chesterfield had gone.

Essex were the visitors the following season when there was a very painful experience for an umpire.

> I also remember a funny incident at Queen's Park, although it was not very funny for me. Derbyshire had a fine bowler in Dallas Moir, a big slow left-arm bowler from Scotland. It pains me every time I think about him. Moir was the chap who bowled a longhop to South African Ken McEwan batting for Essex at the time. McEwan was one of the hardest strikers of the ball in the game, and he pulled it towards me at square leg. It struck me on the shin, and I thought he had broken my leg. As I went down clutching my leg it came up like a football before my eyes which were watering ever so much. Moir came over, stooped down, picked me up in his arms as if I were no more than a little baby, carried me off to the physio's room, and laid me ever so gently down on the treatment table. I have still got a lump on my shin today and that was a long time ago. (Dickie Bird)

> Chesterfield is actually my favourite cricket ground in England (when the sun shines). I made two debuts there, one for Derbyshire, which was my first-class debut back in 1982, against the Pakistani touring team and the other for Durham County Cricket Club in a Championship match against Derbyshire in 1994. I remember both for massively different reasons; obviously my first-class debut for Derbyshire was always going to be a nervous affair, but a game that, as a schoolboy, you hoped that one day you might have the chance to play. I remember getting off the mark with a

straight drive down the ground off Muddassar Nazar which went
for four. I only got six in the first innings and 12 in the second, but
loved every minute of it. I also remember Zaheer Abbas getting a
big hundred in their second innings and thinking to myself what a
great player he was. We lost the game comfortably, but it had been
a marvellous three days for me just being on a cricket field with all
those great players. (John Morris)

Also playing for the Pakistanis were Imran Khan and Abdul Qadir.
   Two years later Devon Malcolm made his debut at Chesterfield.

He meandered up to bowl and his first over had 11 balls. That was
before they discovered that he was wearing the wrong glasses!
(David Griffin)

1985 was not the most successful of seasons. After two days in which
Derbyshire were comprehensively outplayed by Leicestershire, Derbyshire's
total stood at 149 for six still 54 runs away from making Leicestershire bat
again. It was expected that the match would soon be over and it was decided
that no admission charge would be made on the final day. Paul Newman had
other ideas as he made 115 before being last out when the total was 323 (his
previous highest score was 56) and the match was extended until late in the
afternoon.

   The following season a furious assault by Allan Warner, batting at

25. The pavilion in the late 1980s, flanked by press/score box to the right and the terraces to the
left, both of which were removed during the restoration. (Janet Murphy)

number seven against Leicestershire, brought him 81 off 63
balls before he realised that he
was on course for a century;
the next ten runs took 27 balls
and then he was out. (Janet
Murphy)

With a small ground and quick
pitch, there tend to be lots of
boundaries and lots of wickets
at Chesterfield. When Derbyshire played Lancashire in
1989, Lancashire were soon 14
for two. Neil Fairbrother was
floored by a bouncer from Ian
Bishop. His response was to
score 161 in next to no time.
The rest of the batting folded
and they were all out before
tea. (Tim Kemp)

26. Poised for action during the first match of
the season in 1987. Left to right Roger Finney,
Bernie Maher and Bruce Roberts. Roberts scored
184 on the first day. (Janet Murphy)

His innings included 21 fours and
six sixes. In their second innings
Derbyshire required 220 to win; they
finished 27 runs short with two wickets left. Rather overshadowed by
Fairbrother's innings was the performance of the Lancashire wicket-keeper,
Warren Hegg, who took 11 catches to equal the world record.

Just over two weeks later the match was against Yorkshire. By coincidence
this time Derbyshire needed 219 to win, which they did with three wickets in
hand. It was a memorable match. Although Derbyshire had beaten Yorkshire in
one-day games at Chesterfield, most notably in 1986 when they won by ten
wickets with 11 overs to spare, and they had defeated Yorkshire in the
Championship in 1983 and 1986 in Yorkshire, this was the first time they had
beaten them in Derbyshire since 1957. Even better, they won the Refuge
Assurance Sunday League game as well.

I had been watching Derbyshire for years before I saw them beat
Yorkshire whether in the Championship or a one-day game. Our
daughter brought our grand-daughter to the cricket when she was
just three-weeks-old. In the next few days she 'saw' Derbyshire
beat Yorkshire in the Championship and the Sunday League, and I
had waited for years. (John Redhead)

27. 18-year-old Ian Bishop, in his first season for Derbyshire and 19-year-old Chris Adams, in his second season, leave the field after a stand of 50 which saw Derbyshire safely home. (Janet Murphy)

The high reputation of the pitches continued through the 1970s and 80s under Doxey Walker who won the Groundsman of the Year award for out grounds four times and was runner-up on several other occasions. As well as preparing the pitch he played, umpired and helped develop young players.

> He was really dedicated and loved his work. When the weather was a problem he used to stay in the Park until midnight and next morning he was up again at 6 a.m. and ringing the weather centre for the forecast. (Margaret Walker)

> I was watching Doxey Walker supervising the ground staff mopping up using a 'whale' borrowed from Abbeydale Park. A Yorkshireman sitting next to me made some disparaging remark about the ground staff at these smaller grounds. His companion pointed out that Doxey Walker had just won Groundsman of the Year award. The Yorkshireman's grudging response was that he supposed he must be all right if the groundsman at Abbeydale was prepared to lend him his equipment! (Janet Murphy)

28. The groundsman's job can be a lonely one. Doxey Walker applies the light roller, which is still in use today. (Peter Joy)

The following year there were two completely contrasting innings.

> India's master batsman Sachin Tendulkar stood at the side of me in the middle during a tourist match at Queen's Park, Chesterfield and reflected: 'Do you know Dickie, I don't think I have ever seen a more beautiful cricket ground and setting than this.' As we looked out past the flowers in full bloom, through the archway of trees in all their greenery to the famous crooked spire of St Mary's and All Saints Church, I had to agree with him. In its pomp in the middle of summer, there is no more picturesque ground in the world. (Dickie Bird)

17-year-old Tendulkar was enjoying himself making 105 not out as he steered India to victory with two balls to spare in a 55 overs a side game. He hit one ball clean out of the ground.

A few weeks later it was the turn of Andy Brown.

> Andy Brown batted for hours to reach a century against Northants. He was in the nineties for three-quarters of an hour. When he

reached 139 a ball from Curtly Ambrose broke his finger[1] and he had to retire hurt. He didn't play again that season. (Tim Kemp)

There was only one Refuge Assurance Sunday League match at Chesterfield that year and it was a high scoring game. Kent made 276 for four and Derbyshire knocked the runs off, with ten balls and six wickets to spare, with Kim Barnett leading the way with 127 off 101 balls. It was the year that Derbyshire won the Refuge Assurance Sunday League title with Ole Mortensen's niggardly bowling an important factor. In this match he took nought for 23 in his eight overs.

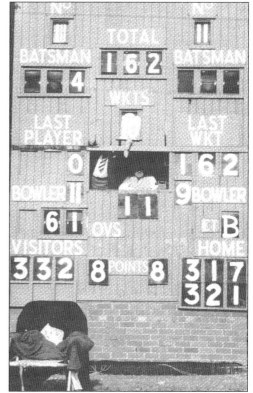

In 1991 we played Hampshire on what proved a crumbly Weetabix of a pitch, a real 'Bunsen burner' and a complete aberration from the normal quick bouncy pitches we have come to expect from Queen's Park. Things started ominously with Chris Smith and

29. The scoreboard operators relax after a good day's work. Derbyshire beat Yorkshire by 144 runs in 1990, with Geoff Miller taking six for 45 on the final day. (Ken Roe)

Kevin James both scoring hundreds and yet, as the pitch deteriorated, Hampshire fell for 258. It is, I think, a record for the lowest team score in England in which two players have made hundreds. (Tim O'Gorman, *Chesterfield Cricket Club: 100 Years at Queen's Park*)

A third successive victory over Yorkshire at Chesterfield in the last match of the season resulted in Derbyshire finishing in third place in the championship.

There was a remarkable innings by Chris Adams in 1992 in the Sunday League. Although starting slowly, he scored 141 not out off 102 balls with ten sixes and seven fours.

Kent were on the receiving end and by the finish their bowlers were applauding their own efforts if they managed to bowl a dot ball. (Tim O'Gorman, *Chesterfield Cricket Club: 100 Years at Queen's Park*)

---

[1] The ball shattered the knuckle of the first finger of his left hand.

Devon Malcolm caught one six on the pavilion balcony. (David Griffin)

By now the way in which cricket was financed was changing with sponsorship becoming increasingly important.

> I was walking through the Park one day when there were several cricket 'matches' in progress on the ground each with one batsman, a bowler, and several fielders, mostly in suits, but with a few Derbyshire players, including Michael Holding, amongst them. When I enquired what was happening I was told that this was a 'thank you' from Derbyshire to businessmen who had supported the Club during the season. Imagine going to work next morning and telling your colleagues that you had been batting against Michael Holding! (Janet Murphy)

Gone were the days when Derbyshire paid the Council for the occasions when the Park was closed to the public during cricket matches; instead the Council was grant aiding the club, as were other councils. Between 1983 and 1992 Championship matches were played at Buxton, Heanor and Ilkeston and one-day games at places such as Leek, Cheadle and Knypersley. At the end of the 1992 season the policy changed and, when the fixture list for the following season was announced, all games were to be played at Derby apart from a four-day game (three days of which were washed out) and a one-day game against Yorkshire at Chesterfield.

Once again there were fears for the future of cricket at Chesterfield.

> We started a Keep Cricket at Chesterfield campaign. We wrote letters to the *Wisden Cricket Monthly*, the *Derby Evening Telegraph*, and the *Derbyshire Times* and collected about 1,000 signatures on a petition. (David Griffin)

The campaign received international publicity.

> I was in Madras for the Test match and was amazed when this banner appeared in the lunch interval. (Trevor Bowring)

> The photograph was taken in Madras in 1993 at a Test Match between England and India. I painted the banner in a Madras hotel bedroom using a tin of paint and some white cloth which we bought at the market there. At the time my partner, Ruth Donnelly, and I were migrating to Australia and stopped off to watch the cricket. We also went to a local bakery in Madras and asked them

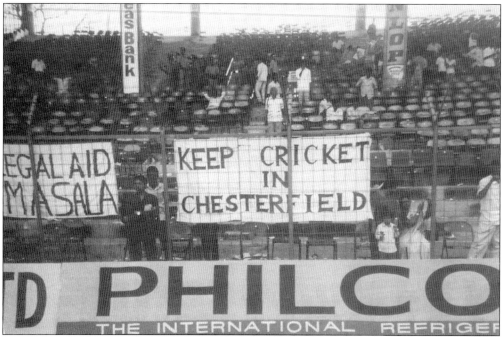

30. Madras, 1993. (Trevor Bowring)

> to bake a chocolate cake with the slogan 'Keep cricket in
> Chesterfield' written in icing. We presented this cake to Brian
> Johnston and talked to him about the possible loss of county
> cricket from Queen's Park. He mentioned the cake and the banner
> during the BBC Test Match Special commentary. (Tommy Leonard)

Although the following season there were again 11 days cricket at Chesterfield, increasingly there were concerns about the outdated nature of the
facilities in the Park. With the adoption of compulsory competitive tendering
in the early nineties the maintenance of Queen's Park was carried out by
external contractors. At the end of the contract the staff were transferred back
to the Leisure Services Department. Tim Nicholls remained the groundsman
throughout.

> I joined the Parks Department in 1979 and worked on the pitches
> away from Queen's Park although, if there were county matches on
> and Doxey Walker was short-handed, I used to help him so I knew
> the ground. Doxey was followed by Ian Whibberley and Billy
> Gillette until I moved to the Park in 1993, working with the
> experienced Roy Goodyear (brother of Walter) who had worked on
> the pitches for many years. You really have to be happy in your
> work because being a groundsman can be lonely. (Tim Nicholls)

My second debut at Chesterfield was entirely different affair as I
left Derbyshire at the end of the 1993 season and had joined
Durham for the start of the 1994 season. How ironic that the
fixtures put me back to my favourite ground to play against my
former county. We batted first on a great pitch for batting and
scored over 600 with Mark Saxelby scoring a brilliant 181. I was
desperately disappointed not to score my first hundred for
Durham when I was caught by Chris Adams off Phil DeFreitas for
90. Derbyshire were made to follow-on, but in the second innings
Mohammad Azharuddin scored a truly breathtaking 205 before I
caught him at mid-on off Phil Bainbridge. The quality of Azza's
innings was unbelievable and it set up a nasty little chase for us of
around 160 on the last afternoon which we achieved in the end
quite comfortably. Funny how things stick in your mind though, on
the Sunday, whilst we were chasing the winning runs, news came
through of the death of Ayrton Senna, the great Brazilian Formula
One racing driver, and I remember feeling quite saddened by that
news. (John Morris)

Mohammad Azharuddin was dropped before scoring. Despite his innings,
which included 21 fours and six sixes, Durham won by seven wickets.

Three months later it was the turn of another world-class batsman — Brian
Lara.

I only had one game in Queen's Park. The pitch was a bit green
and Devon Malcolm was bowling fast. Brian advanced down the
wicket to his first ball from Malcolm and smashed it through extra
cover for four. The faster Devon bowled, the quicker the ball went
to the boundary. He had three men out for the hook shot, but Brian
kept dispatching the ball to the spaces between them. It was
awesome. (Dougie Brown)

Lara raced to a century before lunch on the first day as he made 142; he made a
rapid 51 in the second innings. His performance eclipsed that of the
Warwickshire wicket-keeper Keith Piper whose seven victims in Derbyshire's
second innings gave him a total of 11 dismissals for the match.

A year later there was a match of complete contrast as Yorkshire beat
Derbyshire by seven runs in a low scoring match which was reminiscent of the
one in 1914 as Derbyshire lost five wickets for one run in their second innings
with Hartley taking nine for 41.

One of my very first matches for Yorkshire Seconds was against
Derbyshire at Queen's Park. The pitch was quick and superb for

batting and the outfield was lightning fast. At close of play on the first day I was 96 not out. The whole of my family turned up to see me score my first century the next day, however, unfortunately, I was caught behind from the very first ball of the day. Never mind, they still had a great day out at one of the best venues for county cricket in the country.

My next outing at Queen's Park in county cricket was as 12th man for Yorkshire. One of our players was off the field injured, so I had to field for most of both of Derbyshire's innings. It just so happened that it was the match in which my now fellow First-class Umpire Peter Hartley took nine second innings Derbyshire wickets to win the match for Yorkshire. I believe that it was not too long after this match that county cricket was taken away from Chesterfield. This was especially disappointing at the time as two of my favourite grounds when I was growing up no longer hosted first-class county cricket — Queen's Park and Abbeydale Park in Sheffield. (Richard Kettleborough)

Ian Blackwell made his debut for Derbyshire in 1997 two days before his 19th birthday.

I only managed to play one game as a professional at Queen's Park, but I will remember it for the rest of my life. I made my Sunday League debut against Hampshire, scoring 29 and helping Derbyshire to win the game. (Ian Blackwell)

1998 was the centenary of first-class cricket in the park. It should have been a time of celebration. A centenary dinner was held on the eve of the match against Leicestershire, which was a good contest, but the match against Gloucestershire was a dismal affair. The first day was washed out, Gloucestershire batted until lunch on the third day making a draw the most likely result and only the diehard supporters stayed to the bitter end. The Sunday match was washed out.

Two weeks later the blow fell.

Derbyshire County Cricket Club announced that they would no longer play at Chesterfield citing the low crowds and the cost of playing at Chesterfield as the main reasons. Although supporters were aware that relations between the club and the Council had deteriorated it was a devastating blow. The club lost a substantial amount of support, and the Council lost an attraction at a time when tourism was becoming increasingly important in the town, but the biggest losers were the cricket fans of north Derbyshire and south Yorkshire.

Prominent in the fight to keep cricket at Chesterfield in the 1980s were Les Hart, Brian Holling and Ken Roe, stalwarts from the Chesterfield Cricket

Lovers' Society, who also served on the Derbyshire Committee and were familiar to the supporters as operators of the public address system.

I became a member of the Matlock Regional Council of the Derbyshire County Cricket Club and the Chesterfield Cricket Lovers', as well as serving on the Derbyshire Committee for 29 years, most of them as Ground Committee Chairman. Because of this I had many enjoyable years with many friends trying to encourage the County Club to keep first-class cricket at Queen's Park with the co-operation of the Chesterfield Borough Council and the Chesterfield Cricket Club.

My friends and I spent many years helping with the preparation of pitches etc. with the energetic Chesterfield ground staff and, because of my involvement with the public address, repairing and installing the speakers and telephone with connections through the trees to the little scorer's hut and to the scoreboard. We managed to keep the scoreboard working (after spells of vandalism). We also enjoyed days painting the seats, putting up advertising boards and trying to keep the toilets tidy!

We spent much time trying to keep the ducks and geese off the playing area.

31. Rain stopped play. In the background is the now demolished A.G.D. building. (Ken Roe)

As many of you know we ran the public address system from the upstairs room behind the wall clock — I remember one occasion when the wiring to the output horns got damaged and I circulated the ground with a hand-held notice board telling spectators about the team changes. This reminds me of another occasion when, prior to the start of a match against Yorkshire, I was debarred by the then captain from entering the away team dressing-room to ascertain team changes before we had team sheets duplicated at Robinsons down the road.

One year Stan Tacey was in the scorers' hut some 100 yards east of the pavilion and he rang me up to say his electrics had failed and he could not get through to Leeds to furnish the match information to the radio and TV people. Guess who had pulled out the plug out of the connection in the home dressing room in the pavilion — he's now a leading player at Sussex!

At Queen's Park it was often useful for the PA to see who had his pads on ready to go out to the square at the fall of the next wicket so that we could introduce the new batsman over the PA. I saw a padded-up figure leave the balcony when the wicket fell, but unfortunately, after I'd introduced him over the PA, he turned round to show me that his skin was of a different colour!

Another funny episode at Queen's Park was when we had a wasps' nest inside the roof at our end of the pavilion. I have never seen radio commentators move so quickly.

There was also another PA bloomer when, with wickets of the opposition falling quite quickly, I saw some people standing in front of the sight screen at the lake end — I asked them to move 'before we take the next wicket'. (Ken Roe)

I remember Douglas Carr asking someone to remove their 'Cord Fortina'. The players fell about laughing. (Edwin Smith)

4   The spectators

During the time I played at Queen's Park I always found the crowd knowledgeable and appreciative. It was a sad day when first-class cricket was stopped and I'm very pleased it's back. (Harold Rhodes)

My earliest memory of watching cricket at Queen's Park was nearly 70 years ago when I cycled from my home (in Alfreton then) to a match there and left my cycle by the spiked railings at the North side of the ground. When the match was over I climbed over the railings, but unfortunately drove a spike through my upper right thigh. Stupidly I still cycled home down the slopes and up the hills, and finished up at our local doctor's for stitching. In those days at Queen's Park we often ran to retrieve the ball from the brook at the bottom end. (Ken Roe)

The gates to the Park were normally locked on cricket match days and entrance to the Park was through the two turnstiles, one on Boythorpe Road and the other on Park Road. Hessian cloth was hung on the doors or gates to stop anyone seeing the activity taking place on the cricket pitch. Also park rangers and extra ones on match days patrolled the perimeter of the Park to prevent possible spectators from climbing over the wall. A favourite point was the junction of Park Road and Boythorpe Avenue for enterprising boys to get over the wall, helping each other and disappearing into the crowd. If they got caught, they got kicked out, but many a time they made it. (Ken Silcock)

I have many happy memories of watching cricket in the sylvan setting of the Park, dating back to the early 1950s when, as a boy living near Derby, I watched my father, Sergeant Harold Hartley, playing for the county police in matches against other forces on the Queen's Park pitch. (Roger Hartley)

The Grammar School was within easy access of Queen's Park. After school a quick dash through town was made to try and catch as much play as possible. Schoolboys paid one shilling (pre-decimal terms) to obtain access to the playing area. It was good value to watch some three hours of cricket and was part of

32. Steven Mallender, with the West Indians, including Clive Lloyd, warming up in the background. (Mrs Mallender)

growing up, a way of life; an opportunity to learn the many facets and skills of the game. At close of play came the chance to catch a glimpse of your heroes and to ask politely for coveted signatures in autograph books. In those days cricketers would not sign until the close of play. (W. Leverton in *Derbyshire County Cricket Year Book*, 1999)

Barry Richards refused to autograph an article about himself because he didn't like the journalist. (David Griffin)

When the West Indians came in 1963 drizzle delayed the start of play. Wes Hall gave catching practice to a group of boys and when he got tired of that he spent about twenty minutes signing autographs. (Janet Murphy)

About thirty years ago I took one of my sons to watch the West Indians playing Derbyshire. Unfortunately Steven was taken ill during the day and he was taken into the holy-of-holies, the pavilion office, to wait for a taxi to come to take him home — a day never to be forgotten. (Mrs Mallender)

At Chesterfield you are always close to the action.

Tommy Mitchell, the famous spin bowler, went on the famous 'Bodyline' tour of Australia in 1932–3 with Douglas Jardine, but he never played in a Test, because they did not need him, only Larwood and Voce. This match was being played in the Park. Mitchell was fielding at long leg near the Park Road entrance. Derbyshire were unable to get the batsman out and a spectator shouted to Tommy: 'I will give you a spice[1] if you can get him out!' Anyway next over Mitchell bowled at the offending batsman and bowled him first ball. Whilst waiting for the new batsman to arrive at the wicket, Tommy came over to the spectator and said: 'Where's my spice?' What a character. (Ken Silcock)

[1] A sweet.

33. A study in concentration at the match against the West Indians in 1957. (*Derbyshire Countryside*)

I was bowling at the lake end and it was a very hot day; we didn't have people bringing drinks out to us like they do today. When I was fielding at fine leg a retired miner said: 'Tha looks a bit thirsty lad'. He bought a pint of bitter and kept it under his seat for me to have a drink at the end of each over. (Brian Jackson)

I was sitting at the lake end with my six-year-old son. Derek Underwood was fielding in front of us. My son tapped him on the leg and asked if he would like a sweet. Underwood thanked him and was given an Opal Fruit. (John Bolton)

When just a little older and by then a keen Derbyshire supporter, I became a 'regular' and used to get most upset if family holidays abroad coincided with Derbyshire fixtures in Chesterfield (in those days the County used to play at least six three-day matches per season in the Park). On trips to the cricket my parents took great delight in recounting to their friends how they were obliged to seek accommodation for the afternoon on the uncomfortable benches at the lake end, whilst the 'young squire' was making full use of his

Junior Member's ticket (for which they had paid) to join his fellow 'toffs' in the sanctuary of the pavilion, emerging only at tea time upon spotting the opening of the parental picnic hamper in the far distance.

Sometimes, of course, the cricket would pass through a quiet, soporific phase, at which point we would produce our own bat and ball and provide our own cricketing entertainment. It was one such occasion played out on the area of grass between the old (now demolished) refreshment kiosk and the tents on the bank that gave rise to the now notorious episode of the sausage roll. I was fielding at mid-on and simultaneously assuaging my lunchtime hunger pangs when I was unexpectedly called into action by a lofted ball hit in my direction. In my confusion — and to the dismay of the bowler, Martin Willows, I managed to drop the ball whilst clinging on with grim determination to my sausage roll. A further question mark was raised as to my commitment to the cause and to the team ethic when I paused to take a large bite out of the sausage roll before turning to amble reluctantly after the fast disappearing ball, runs meanwhile accruing remorselessly to the batsman's score. Martin has never allowed me to forget this less than glorious incident in my cricket career. (John Cook)

Not only is Queen's Park a fantastic place to play, the feel of the ground is awesome. Watching there is such a pleasure and never fails to attract families and fathers with their kids whilst they play in the Park. I saw some fantastic players there over the years, Brian Lara, Graeme Hick, Tom Moody and of course some Derbyshire greats too, Chris Adams, Dean Jones, Phil DeFreitas, John Morris and Devon Malcolm to mention just a few. (Ian Blackwell)

My father always used to come to the matches when I was playing. He might even have been the gentleman who waved his stick in the direction of Sid Buller when Rhodes was no-balled for throwing. I always told him not to come near the dressing-room. One day I was having a shower when there was a knock on the dressing-room door and he asked: 'Is Brian there? Somebody has pinched his car.' It turned up six weeks later down a track in Sherwood Forest with no more damage than a flat battery. (Brian Jackson)

I came from London in February 1967 to live at Loundsley Green in Chesterfield and to work at the Accountant General's Department of the Post Office, which overlooked Queen's Park. Two attractions

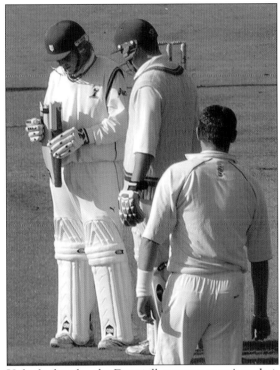

Unlucky break – the Dunstall openers examine a bat broken by a ball from Chesterfield's Michael Deane. (Mike Taylor)

Men at work – preparing the pitch for a Chesterfield match. (Mike Taylor)

The latter half of June 2007 was notable for the heavy rain which fell culminating in the flooding of June 25th. Fortunately this storm passed by and the spectators at the Graeme Welch benefit match were lucky to escape a soaking. (Janet Murphy)

A section of the crowd at the Derbyshire v Durham match Pro 40 League match September 2007. (John Smith – Chesterfield Borough Council)

immediately became inspirational, the Crooked Spire and Queen's Park. I have visited the Park on many occasions as a player, cricket coach and spectator to watch Derbyshire. (Richard Suttle)

Richard Suttle is a familiar figure around Chesterfield. He was very involved in the setting up of the AGD Junior Cricket Club, many of whose players have gone on to play in the Park for different teams. In addition, members of Chesterfield Cricket Club have joined tours that he has organised to Barbados.

> My very first memory of Queen's Park in Chesterfield was as a young boy with a cricket bat under one arm and a football under the other going along with my dad, who at the time was playing for Steetley in the Bassetlaw League. I remember him telling me that Chesterfield were a good side with the likes of Harry Cartwright and Andy Bowers being the major players.
>
> Chesterfield was the away fixture that all the other children, myself included, looked forward to most of all in the season. Not only were we taken aback by how stunning the ground was but also because there was lots of space to play cricket and football to our hearts' content. There was also the famous boating lake and ice-cream kiosk. We spent many a happy Saturday afternoon on that lake and certainly on one occasion a couple of us had to be helped from the water after a childish prank had gone very wrong.
>
> I also saw some of my first county cricket at Queen's Park. I remember going with my dad to watch Derbyshire play. Derbyshire had some fine players then with the likes of Peter Kirsten and Geoff Miller, but the one abiding memory I have of those visits was of the great Michael Holding in full flow from the pavilion end; a magnificent sight that I can still picture to this day. Thankfully I was not batting against him at the time! (Richard Kettleborough)

The spectators who watch Chesterfield Cricket Club may not be as numerous, but they still take a keen interest.

> It was my first game as the new Chesterfield captain and I wanted to sparkle. It was not to be because after the first ball the scoreboard read 0-1. Five minutes later I was stalking round the Queen's Park ground after having been given out to a catch which bounced in front of first slip. My thunderous and ill-tempered walk took me past a group of old lads who used to sit on the right side of the pavilion and although they were staunch Chesterfield supporters, they never overlooked the chance to poke fun at our players — particularly the new captain out for a duck. Five

34. A popular vantage point during the Derbyshire v Surrey Pro 40 League match in 2006. In the summer months the Crooked Spire is barely visible above the trees. (John Smith – Chesterfield Borough Council)

minutes after a duck is never the time to speak to me and for that matter I'm not really in a cheerful humour five minutes after any end of innings. After playful banter between us — mine conducted through a forced smile and clenched teeth — one of them said: 'What's a ruddy Yorkshireman doing captaining Chesterfield anyway?' To which I answered: 'I'm doing missionary work trying to teach you Derbyshire Tups about fair play'. Thinking I'd won that round I turned in triumph to resume my walk only to hear someone to shout after me: 'Tha' might know about cricket, but tha's geography is no good — these boggers come from Nottinghamshire.' My grandfather always said that if you wanted a fool in Derbyshire, you had to take one with you, and he was right as these old lads constantly proved to me. (Clive Baxter, *Chesterfield Cricket Club: 100 Years at Queen's Park*)

5 Chesterfield Cricket Club, 1946-2007

For Chesterfield Cricket Club league cricket began again in 1946 and shortly afterwards the club became the one with the longest continual membership in the Derbyshire League.

> On a Saturday possibly in 1945 or 1946 Geoff Atrill was batting at the lake end against a local colliery side. The fast bowler bowled, Geoff mis-hit the ball and it flew off the top of the bat and hit short leg on the head, the ball flew back in the air and the wicket-keeper promptly caught it. The stumper appealed for a catch and the umpire quite rightly gave him out caught behind. Meanwhile the short leg was unconscious on the pitch. Geoff departed into the pavilion followed by the cricketers carrying their team mate. An ambulance was called and he was taken to the Royal Hospital. (Ken Silcock)

> I was playing for Chesterfield Cricket Club against the Paladins, a touring side from Durham. I ran into bowl and hit the batsman on the leg plumb lbw. 'Not out' said the umpire (a Durham man). The same thing happened with the next ball — not out again! When it happened a third time I didn't bother to appeal, thinking that the umpire was never going to give him out. 'Why didn't you appeal?' he said: 'I would have given him out.' (Brian Austin)

An important part of Derbyshire's success in the 1950s was the wicket-keeping of George Dawkes, supported by the close catchers Donald Carr, Derek Morgan and Alan Revill. For Chesterfield Cricket Club it was the famous combination of George Lowe and Arthur Revill in the slips with Bob Naylor behind the stumps that was particularly renowned for its catching and little got past them. The First Eleven won the Derbyshire League six times in ten seasons between 1947 and 1957. In 1953 the First Eleven won the Rayner Cup and the Second Eleven won the Spriggs Memorial Cup as Division 3 Champions. The First Eleven won the League Championship in 1955, overtaking Morton, who had led the table for most of the season, in the last match. Sent in to bat against Staveley Welfare, Chesterfield were 19 for six at one stage, but reached a total of 92 thanks to G.S. Rodgers who scored 67; they won the Championship by one point. The Second Eleven again won the Division 3 Championship. During the three seasons since joining the division in 1952 the Second Eleven had played 60 matches and lost just two. Champions again in the following two seasons the First Eleven then left the Derbyshire League, of which they had been members since 1893, to face the stronger challenge of the Bassetlaw League, which included teams from Derbyshire, Nottinghamshire, Yorkshire and Lincolnshire. They moved up from Division 1C to 1A in two seasons.

Captain throughout this successful period, from 1939 to 1959, was Geoff Atrill. F.C. (Jim) Brailsford joined the Club when he was 14. Two years later he was a regular with the Chesterfield First Eleven and the Derbyshire Second Eleven. He took over the captaincy between 1960 and 1964 after several successful years with the First Eleven and one season with Derbyshire before having a spell as a professional in the Bradford League.

Other Chesterfield players who played for Derbyshire at this time were George Lowe and David Short. George Lowe also captained the Derbyshire Second Eleven.

> I used to spend all my holidays playing cricket, the wife was very good and took the children to the seaside whilst I played cricket. (George Lowe)

> I remember when I was about 14 taking seven for 11 bowling leg-breaks and googlies for a Chesterfield Wednesday side. (David Short)

35. Chesterfield First XI August 1947. *Standing:* A Glover, L. Bargh, F. Bell, A. Revill, B. Stilgow, G. Lowe, J. Hirst, S. Cantrill (Secretary). *Seated:* A. Frisby, G. Bush, R. Naylor, G. Atrill, D. Moore, J. Enion, B. Cantrill (Scorer). Frisby is kneeling on his collecting box. (G. Lowe)

A familiar figure around the ground at this time was 'Frisby'.

> For years 'Frisby' travelled round the ground at cricket matches collecting monies for both Derbyshire County Cricket Club and Chesterfield Cricket Club in his famous white coat. Towards the end he got very bad on his feet, but he was a very good servant to both these organisations. I can hear his call now: 'Scorecards 3d. Fall of last wicket'. There was a printing press in the pavilion and the scorecards were kept up to date, plus the stop press of the *Star* was printed there so the followers knew the winner of the latest race at Doncaster for example, and the starting price etc. I used to wait until very late on the third day when it was possible to buy a scorecard completed for almost the whole match. (Ken Silcock)

Another member of the Pope family played at Queen's Park, Alf's son, Tony.

> I was well into my forties before I got a chance to play in Queen's Park. This was only because Jim Brailsford stood down in a friendly match against a touring team so that I could play. It was not until the advent of the Derbyshire Cup in the late seventies that any cricketers from Derby got the chance to play on the Park. We had all watched Derbyshire play there, but as Chesterfield were in the Bassetlaw League, and no Derby-based teams were, none of us had the chance to play there. (Tony Pope)

36. Chesterfield U14, 1970 – five of this team played first eleven cricket for Chesterfield. (Peter Joy)

My first ever game on Queen's Park was for the first club I ever played for my 'home' club Killamarsh, who were captained by the former Derbyshire and England player Cliff Gladwin, a real 'character', who taught me a lot about cricket and added a quite a few new words to my vocabulary! We were playing against Chesterfield in the Bassetlaw League Division 1A and were skittled out for just 28 on a particularly 'green' and lively pitch by the bowling of Andy Bowers, Alan Bonsall and David Webster as I remember. I didn't make many — obviously! In an epic match Chesterfield knocked off the runs for the loss of seven wickets. Their number ten batsman Stuart Gregory had gone home after tea so they only had Alan Bonsall to come in as last man! (Harry Cartwright)

Captain that day was Ralph Brailsford, brother of Jim, who returned to the club in 1973 and was captain of the First Eleven for a second spell from 1975 to 1981. He recruited many existing and former first-class players to his side including off-spinner Edwin Smith. During each of the three seasons Smith was with Chesterfield he topped the Bassetlaw League averages. Chesterfield Cricket Club was a strong force in the Bassetlaw League during this period, but never won the Championship title, despite coming very close. They were runners-up five times in six seasons between 1977 and 1982. In 1979 they were runners-up to the Nottinghamshire Second Eleven, with several professionals in the side. A year later they failed by one run to get a fourth point which would have given the Championship. In 1981, Jim Brailsford's last season as captain, they were winners of the Harry Tomlins Trophy (the Bassetlaw League 40-over knock-out cup which they had first won in 1978) for the second successive year and the Derbyshire Cup. Chesterfield took part in this 60-over competition by invitation; they were winners in 1977, 1981, 1982, and 1983.

Clive Baxter became captain in 1982 and the destination of the Championship was determined in a 'final ball of the season' thriller against Bridon Cricket Club. Chesterfield needed only a draw to win the Championship. With just two overs left Bridon wanted 25 runs and their number 11 was at the wicket.

Our penultimate over was a nightmare. It cost us 18 runs which included three no-balls and three dropped catches in the deep. The last over was to be bowled by Andy Bowers and by this time the light was really bad, as it often is in matches played in September. Bridon scrambled three runs off Andy's first five balls, setting the scene for the last ball of the season. They now needed four runs to win and with very bad light, the field spread far and wide, and Paddy Phelan (not the best batsman in the world) to face, I was convinced that Chesterfield was going to win its first Bassetlaw Division 1 title. Andy could have bowled a variety of balls, but he decided that Paddy was not the bravest player of the bouncer, even if he could see it in the dark. And seeing that the wicket-keeper was three-quarters of the way to the boundary anyway, it seemed like a sound idea. Last ball of the season and the title depended on it. Andy bounced Paddy, who will say that he kept his eye on the ball, as he played back and pulled the ball for four and a famous victory. What really happened was that Paddy closed his eyes and thought of Bridon — wafted his bat as much in self-defence as in anger — top-edged the ball that he could never really have seen — and diverted it in a gentle arc tantalisingly just over the head of the wicket-keeper who was standing 30 yards from the wicket. That moment summed up for me all the drama and uncertainty of cricket and as I walked off the field to shake the hand of their captain and to congratulate him on winning the Championship, I had just 30 seconds to put on a brave face. (Clive Baxter in *Chesterfield Cricket Club: 100 Years at Queen's Park*)

Also playing for Chesterfield at this time was the West Indian Delroy Morgan who went on to captain Jamaica.

Clive Baxter rang me one morning to say there was a mid-week friendly at Ashover and the team was a bowler short. I suggested Delroy who was an occasional bowler for Chesterfield and was available. On arrival at Ashover Clive asked if he could bat. 'He opens the batting for Jamaica' I replied. Delroy opened the batting and by lunch was in the 90s. 'Get your hundred and then get out' Clive instructed Delroy who thought he said: 'Hit out' and proceeded to thrash the opposing bowlers to all parts of Ashover. Clive was not amused and neither were the opposition who quashed any thoughts of a repeat fixture the following year. (Peter Joy)

The last time that Chesterfield won the Derbyshire Cup was in 1983. Our opponents in the final, played at Queen's Park, were a strong Langley Mill side captained by Tony Borrington and including Bruce Roberts. Despite losing Ted Hemsley and Harry Cartwright early on Chesterfield reached 218 for six off their 60 overs. When they started their reply Borrington was dismissed before a run was scored and they were soon 32 for three with me taking all three for five runs off six overs. Then the spinners took over; Edwin Smith one for 19 off 12; Dave Edmunds one for 14 off 12, and Ted Hemsley one for 12 off six overs; in all the slow bowlers took three for 45 off 30 overs. Although I received the Man of the Match award with four for 31, it was really an all-round team effort. (Andy Bowers)

There was a new captain in 1984, Harry Cartwright, and once more Bridon, who were favourites to win the Championship, were the opponents. At 110 for two Chesterfield were well on the way to victory, but they lost eight wickets for 38 runs and the match was tied.

I've so many fond memories of the 18 years I played for Chesterfield Cricket Club. My association with Chesterfield came about when, in my last season with Derbyshire, I hardly played due to an injury to my Achilles tendon. I eventually had an operation on it and spent about six weeks in a rehabilitation centre called Farnham Park near Slough. It was here that I received a phone call from Jim enquiring if I might be interested in playing for Chesterfield for the next season. When I returned home I was taken out to dinner by Jim and Clive Baxter (the Club Chairman at that time, who sadly died quite recently) who succeeded in persuading me to play for Chesterfield. It was not a difficult decision bearing in mind that it

37. Chesterfield Second XI, 1992 Bassetlaw League Champions *Standing:* C. Jaques, K. Briggs, J. Carley, D. Barnett, M. Barnett, D. Key. *Seated:* I. Blackwell, S. McCarroll, A. Bowers (Captain), S. Bird, J. Blackwell, D. Shannon. (Noëlle McCarroll)

was my favourite ground and that Chesterfield played in the best
league in the area. Probably my most memorable game was against
Langley Mill in the Derbyshire Cup. They had Devon Malcolm
(when he was just starting his Derbyshire career) and Peter Hacker
(the former Nottinghamshire left-arm fast bowler) opening the
bowling. I managed to survive a fiery opening spell from these two
to score 126 not out and regard this as probably my best innings for
Chesterfield on Queen's Park. Another memorable game was
against our 'bitter' rivals Retford. I can't remember our score,
batting first, but it was a good one and the Retford captain, Mike
Hall, obviously decided that it was too many for them to chase.
Retford finished on 40 for six after their full 46 overs which
prompted comments about 'paint drying' and other things!! (Harry
Cartwright)

Yet another member of the Pope family played at Queen's Park in 1994 in
when Chesterfield played the MCC in a match to mark the centenary of cricket
in the park. Tony Pope and his son Tim played for the MCC alongside ex-
Derbyshire players Geoff Miller, Harry Cartwright and Iain Anderson. Despite
a fine all-round performance by Geoff Miller who scored 50, took three for 28

38. The Chesterfield side for the match against the MCC, May 1994. *Standing:* G. Holden, P. Joy,
A. Roach, B. Gladwin, T. Kirk, D. Brightmore, D. Bacon, R. Joy, S. McCarroll, Mayor, Councillor
G. Wright, S. Franks (Scorer), P. Kirk, I. Conroy. *Seated:* A. Bowers, C. Baxter, F.C. Brailsford,
N. Ashley, D. Hopkinson. (*Derbyshire Times*)

39. The MCC side. *Standing:* G. Holden, P. Hampshire, I. Hampshire, I. Anderson, T. Pope, P. Unsworth, A. Boyle, I. Conroy. *Seated:* M.J. Tunaley, G. Miller, H. Cartwright, A.V. Pope, M.H. Chapman. (*Derbyshire Times*)

and made a brilliant catch, Chesterfield, captained by Jim Brailsford, scored 156 to win a rain-curtailed match thanks to Richard Joy's 75 not out and Tim Kirk's three for 26.

Two months later Chris Jacques had a match that he will not forget.

> I joined Chesterfield Cricket Club mainly for the social side, but was often pressed into service when they were a player short. I well remember the match against Blyth. On this occasion I was playing for the Second Eleven, captained by Andy Bowers. It was a sunny July day. Blyth won the toss and elected to bat on a perfect pitch. I opened the bowling with my right-arm trundlers with a young Ian Blackwell bowling at the other end. I got a lot of swing and the wickets fell steadily, helped by a brilliant catch by Darren Barnett. I took two wickets in my sixth over; Ian bowled an over wide of the stumps and had a catch dropped in the slips. Two more wickets fell in my eighth over and then Andy put Kevin Barber, a very occasional bowler, on at the other end. They were all out for 27 and I had taken all ten wickets for 16 runs. As we walked off with everyone applauding, John Blackwell tapped me on the shoulder and said: 'Well done, but you have just spoilt a perfect day'. He was right; we knocked the runs off without loss in just eight overs and the match was over by 4.20 p.m. (Chris Jacques)

THE BASSETLAW AND DISTRICT CRICKET LEAGUE SCORESHEET
sponsored by **Wilkinson** Home and Garden Stores

This form must be completed by the Home Club and sent to the WORKSOP GUARDIAN, WATSON ROAD, WORKSOP, by first-class post and by the earliest collection after the match. The result must also be telephoned to 0773-541-977 by 11 a.m. on the day following the match.

Match CHESTERFIELD v BLYTH played at CHESTERFIELD QUEENS PARK on 9|7| 1994
Innings of BLYTH .... Division 2 Section A Innings of CHESTERFIELD

BATSMAN	HOW OUT	BOWLER	SCORE	BATSMAN	HOW OUT	BOWLER	SCORE
1 T Cockayne	ct + Bowled	C Jacques	2	1 P Boardman	NOT	OUT	9
2 A Edwardson	Bowled	C Jacques	0	2 D Barnett	NOT	OUT	19
3 S Robson	Bowled	C Jacques	3	3 K Briggs	DID NOT BAT		-
4 G Moulds	st M'Carroll	C Jacques	7	4 H Barber	"	"	-
5 T Smith	ct + Bowled	C Jacques	4	5 I Blackwell	"	"	-
6 G Faulkner	ct D Barnett	C Jacques	3	6 J Blackwell	"	"	-
7 W Spence	Bowled	C Jacques	0	7 S Bird	"	"	-
8 D Naghen	ct I Blackwell	C Jacques	0	8 S M'Carroll	"	"	-
9 M Cooper	ct C Briggs	C Jacques	6	9 D Key	"	"	-
10 D Prigmore	NOT	OUT	0	10 C Jacques	"	"	-
11 R Faulkner	LBW	C Jacques	0	11 A Bowers	"	"	-

TOTAL OVERS RECEIVED	14	b 0	lb 0	EXTRAS	2	TOTAL OVERS RECEIVED		b 0	lb 0	EXTRAS	0
WICKETS LOST	10	w 2	nb 0	RUNS	27	WICKETS LOST		w 0	nb 0	RUNS	26

DURATION OF FIRST INNINGS: 1 HR 13 mins DURATION OF SECOND INNINGS: 30 mins 70% target = GAME STARTED AT: 2:30
GAME ENDED AT: 4:20

BOWLER	O	M	R	W	BOWLER	O	M	R	W		
C Jacques	10	3	16	10	M Cooper	4	0	12	0	Result	Bonus
I Blackwell	7	0	6	0	T Smith	3.5	0	16	0	POINTS GAINED: HOME	12
K Barber	2	0	5	0						POINTS GAINED: AWAY	

HOME TEAM'S RECORD TO DATE

PL	12	10	8	6	4	2	0	B.P.	TOTAL POINTS
11	5	0	1	0	3	0	2		80

UMPIRES:
No. 80
No. 140

TO BALANCE: BATSMEN'S RUNS and ALL EXTRAS = RUNS CONCEDED BY BOWLERS + BYES AND LEG BYES

40. The scorecard for Chris Jaques's day of glory. (Chesterfield Cricket Club)

Ian Blackwell has been a prolific scorer for Chesterfield Cricket Club; his innings including a league record-breaking individual score of 213 not out against Bolsover. He had an amazing match on 21 June 1998 when Chesterfield met Quarndon in the Derbyshire Building Society Cup Group B.

> Quarndon batted first and were bowled out for 118 after 54.1 overs. Ian Blackwell had figures of 12-6-12-3, and the experienced Arthur Wragg (3 weeks short of his 57th birthday when the match was played and grandfather of current player Ben Slater) had 12-3-26-2. In reply the first wicket partnership of Ian Blackwell and Mick Barratt put on 111 by the end of the 17th over when Ian was out for 104 off 64 balls with two sixes and 15 fours. Mick Barratt finished with ten not out as Chesterfield finished 119 for one off 19.4 overs. The only Quarndon wicket-taker was Claude Henderson with 6-0-28-1. Claude went on to represent South Africa. (Steve Franks)

In the mid 1990s, the club captaincy transferred to Tim Kirk. The First Eleven won the Harry Tomlins Trophy again in 1995 and 1996. Kirk, Brian Gladwin, Dean Hopkinson, Chris Marples and Simon King formed the backbone of the

First Eleven. The club failed to break the Bassetlaw League duck before it moved to the Derbyshire Premier League in its inaugural season (1999), marking the club's return to a Derbyshire league competition after 41 years in the Bassetlaw League. At the same time the Second Eleven joined the Derbyshire County League.

> When Chesterfield visited Quarndon in 2004, they were second in the Premier League and Chesterfield were languishing near the bottom. Quarndon reached 31 for no wicket without much difficulty and then Simon Lacey came on to bowl. He took seven wickets for 30 as Quarndon were dismissed for 98. Chesterfield went on to win by eight wickets. This remains the best return in the Premier League by a Chesterfield player. (Steve Franks)

41. All eyes follow the ball as Josh Mierkalns of Sawley and Long Eaton hoists his last ball for six. Despite his innings of 137 not out, in a total of 267 for seven, Chesterfield won by five wickets with five balls to spare. (Mike Taylor)

6 Chesterfield Cricket Club today

Chesterfield Cricket Club has been fortunate in the commitment of its officers, following the example of Alderman T.P. Wood who served the club as committee member for 50 years. Serving with him on the committee were M.S. Brodhurst, committee member and president for 50 years, and L. Ludlam, committee member for 35 years.

Such commitment has continued over the years often with sons following fathers with names such as Middleton, Cantrill, Kirk, Joy, Blackwell, Brailsford and Pope recurring.

After the First World War the committee running the club met in the pavilion during the summer and local hostelries during the winter months. Apart from the groundsmen the major problem was the shortage of money with the club borrowing tarpaulins to cover the pitches from the Midland Railway, a motor mower from the Chesterfield Golf Club and a horse from the sewage works. Appeals for money from the County Club and concerns over the size of the overdraft were met by holding whist drives or a dinner. Today the work the committee undertakes is more wide-ranging and involves a great deal more time and effort.

Over recent years there has been a raft of new regulations and requirements affecting cricket clubs many of which need considerable work both in terms of implementation and subsequent maintenance.

While there are invariably good reasons behind these developments, the fact remains that they often impose heavy demands on what is a recreational club run by volunteers whose time and energies are understandably limited by work, family and other interests.

Child protection issues provide a good illustration of these extra demands. Whilst understanding the need for more comprehensive child protection regimes and assurances, the simple fact remains that this need is met by a new layer of policies, practices and procedures which have to be designed and implemented and then monitored and reviewed on a regular basis.

At Chesterfield the work involved in achieving Clubmark accreditation has provided the club with a rigorous standard to work to. It has only been possible due to the outstanding efforts of a volunteer Child Welfare Officer who is competent to undertake the work. Even then the adherence to the standard requires the understanding and support of everyone in the club and has only been possible with the diligent organisation and administration of a volunteer Junior Co-ordinator.

Of course these demands may pose even more challenges for smaller clubs with fewer members to shoulder the workload. However it is not the case that bigger clubs necessarily have a large number of volunteers. Very often a few dedicated volunteers shoulder an undue amount of work and one of the challenges facing many clubs at a time of increasing demands is the enlistment of more volunteers, even if from outside the club.

One common source of volunteers is the pool of former players although Chesterfield as a club is not particularly well endowed in this respect. I suspect that part of the reason for this is that in the past many players joined the club for a period of a few seasons having come from another club before moving on to play out their years somewhere else, often with their original club. Maybe this is in part the reason for me being asked to assume the role as chairman of the club when I have never played for Chesterfield and have only taken an interest in the club since my retirement from work.

Having said that, we are fortunate in having the generous help and support of a small but dedicated group of former players and their families as well as current players. In addition, we are seeing more and more of the parents of our juniors making valuable contributions, so the future for the club is bright given that the work off the field of play is nowadays of fundamental importance to the playing of our wonderful game. (Mike Taylor)

As well as serving on the Club Committee past players have been office holders in the local cricket leagues. Among them Harold Pope, David Mason and Peter Joy were all office-holders for the Bassetlaw League for several years. As well as serving as a member of the Test and County Cricket Board for three years Jim Brailsford served on the Derbyshire County Cricket Club Committee as did others, most notably Edward Mitchell, a committee member for Derbyshire for 40 years as well as chairman and president of Chesterfield Cricket Club, and Frank Hadfield, for several years captain of Chesterfield who also served on Derbyshire's General Committee for ten years.

Jim Brailsford made his debut for Chesterfield at the age of 14 and went on to make at least one appearance at Queen's Park for each of the next 50 years. On 17 August 1997 he faced one delivery and made one not out as Chesterfield declared on 168 for five before bowling the Derbyshire Gentlemen's side out for 102. After the game he was presented with a cut-glass bowl depicting Queen's Park, the Crooked Spire and 50 glorious years. During a long and distinguished career Jim played cricket in 20 countries. Though primarily an opening batsman, one of his most famous achievements was to take the wicket of England captain Ted Dexter with his first ball for Derbyshire. (Fran O'Neill)

Nowadays I have to settle for umpiring in the Park in the Derbyshire Premier League matches, which always brings back happy memories, particularly in the bar after the game. It has always been a friendly place; you regularly find someone wishing to reminisce about the old days. It's always a pleasure to see Jim Brailsford, a stalwart of Chesterfield cricket and a colleague of mine from the 50s. (Harold Rhodes)

42. Harold Rhodes looks on as Ben France bowls. (Mike Taylor)

Jim is one of several players who started their careers with Chesterfield and then went on to play for Derbyshire. Most played just a few games for Derbyshire, but Geoff Miller (254 games) and George Pope (446 games) played many more, as well as playing for England. Ian Blackwell played for Derbyshire for two seasons before he moved to Somerset to further his career and he too played for England. He still retains a keen interest in his home club and has played for them occasionally although his opportunities are limited. Others played for Chesterfield after their Derbyshire careers were over including Harry Cartwright, Simon Lacey and Edwin Smith. Kim Barnett, Mike Hendrick and others played for Chesterfield when not required by Derbyshire. Many others have played for Derbyshire Second Eleven, the Juniors and the Club and Ground. Having played for the Derbyshire Second Eleven for several years Andy Bowers was called into the First Eleven to replace the injured Alan Ward for a one-day game at Edgbaston — the match was abandoned without a ball being bowled. Alan Bonsall suffered in a similar manner.

Jim Brailsford is typical of the players who have stayed on to pass on the benefit of their experience to younger players, whether as captain or coach — people like Andy Bowers, John Blackwell, Tim Kirk and Steve McCarroll.

Each team in the Derbyshire Premier League is allowed to play up to two county-contracted players and there is no limit on the number of professionals who may be used. The present policy of Chesterfield Cricket Club is to spend money on developing young players rather than the employment of expensive overseas players.

The Club had a thriving junior section in the mid-to-late 1980s, but due to the shortage of volunteers to run the sides and lack of support from Chester-field Borough Council (who at that time were not very supportive of junior matches being played on Queen's Park) the club had stopped running junior teams by the start of the 1990s. Steve McCarroll was the prime instigator in the re-launching of a junior section in 1995 by starting an under-12 years side.

> Over the next two years, U13 and U15 teams were added. An U17 team played in 1999, but in subsequent years there were not enough teams to make that age group viable in the Chesterfield and District Youth League. The Derbyshire Premier League then set its expectations of member clubs to start junior cricket at U11 years, so Kwik cricket began at Queen's Park. (Steve McCarroll)

> Over recent years the club has made enormous progress in offering opportunities to youngsters to play cricket. The re-establishment of junior cricket at the club owed much to the commitment of Steve McCarroll in the late 1990s who ran coaching sessions and organised matches for juniors. The junior section of the club has gone from strength to strength over the past ten years and by 2007

the club had teams at U11 Kwik Cricket, U11 hard ball cricket and then at U12, U13, U14, U15 and U17 age levels.

Much of the credit for this progress goes to Andy Brown, who was appointed as club coach in 2003 and who had responsibility for youth development. Andy's outstanding work with the club in all facets was afforded recognition by his appointment to Derbyshire County Cricket Club when he joined John Morris in readiness for the 2008 season.

During his five years with Chesterfield Cricket Club, Andy played a prominent role with juniors at the club by organising coaching sessions and by encouraging club members to go on coaching courses. The increase in qualified coaches enabled further expansion in the provision of opportunities for juniors at the club.

At the same time, Andy made use of funding attracted by the club to deliver coaching opportunities to local schools. In the space of four seasons this community aspect of the club's work has increased dramatically with support from Derbyshire County Council, Derbyshire Sport, Awards for All and more latterly from the Cricket Foundation's 'Chance 2 shine' programme. In 2007, this part of the club's work extended to 23 schools and provided coaching sessions for almost 1,500 youngsters, each attending, on average, nine times.

Over half of the youngsters on the community programme were girls and the resulting demand for girls' cricket soon led to Andy establishing a girls' squad at the club. Within a couple of years the girls were Derbyshire champions and the rapid progress in developing girls' cricket was acknowledged by the ECB when they awarded two women's international matches to the club for 2008.

Andy's departure was always going to present the club with a real challenge in maintaining the momentum. However Simon Mounsey will be continuing with his excellent work as Junior Co-ordinator and this will be of great help to Al Morris who joins the club on his return from Australia in April. (Mike Taylor)

Al Morris played for Chesterfield alongside Geoff Miller and also played a few games for Derbyshire.

I am 16-years-old and have been involved in junior cricket in Queen's Park since I was about seven-years-old. I have always enjoyed being part of Chesterfield Cricket Club and the opportunity this brings of playing on Queen's Park. My first experience of competitive cricket there would have been Kwik cricket (soft ball, plastic bat). I then moved on to hard ball cricket for under-11s at the age of eight or nine. I remember the boundary was always reduced as we were all too small to be able to hit the ball to such a long boundary.

My first senior game in Queen's Park was for the Second Eleven. I was ten-years-old and really only there to make up the numbers, but I managed to take the winning catch with the opposition needing only a few runs to win the game. My team mates were delighted with me and Rob Hiron, who stands at six foot six, ran up and down the pitch with me on his shoulder.

My first game on the Park for the First Eleven was against Denby in 2006 and a fellow junior, Chris Fletcher, and I batted out to save the game for Chesterfield. One of the Denby bowlers, Michael Deane, a former Derbyshire player, now plays for Chesterfield. I finished the game on 15 not out and Chris had 11 not out. (Ben Slater)

Queen's Park is a fantastic ground and will always hold a special place in my heart. My earliest memories would have been when I was ten or 11. I used to go down with my father to watch Derbyshire do battle. I remember playing on the outfield at lunch and tea, pretending to be a professional cricketer and dreaming of playing one day for real. I was also very lucky to play my club cricket there from the age of 12 or 13. (Ian Blackwell)

Queen's Park, Chesterfield holds many wonderful memories for me personally. Playing for Chesterfield Cricket Club as a young teenager and learning the game from such sages as Jim Brailsford, Steve Yates and Alan Bonsall gave me the ideal schooling. Years later I made my county debut for Derbyshire in a one-day game against Kent, and remember walking out to bat, full of pride and extremely nervous.

How times move on. Today I pen this article on the day after I was appointed to be the National Selector of the England Cricket Team. I am an extremely proud man whose roots remain firmly in Chesterfield. The Queen's Park helped me plot my future, and gave me so many opportunities. (Geoff Miller)

Ben Slater's sister Laura also plays cricket.

I decided to play cricket, because I thought 'IF I CAN'T BEAT THEM I WILL JOIN THEM'. I spent a lot of time, watching my brother, Dad and Grandad playing cricket at Queen's Park so I thought I might as well join in. I began by joining the training sessions and was then picked to play Junior Kwik Cricket (soft ball) U11s. I was the only girl to play at that time, but I was made to feel welcome and quickly began to enjoy the game. I now play with Chesterfield for U13s hard ball and I represent Derbyshire Girls at U13s hard ball.

There are now more girl cricketers at Chesterfield, thanks to Andy Brown who started specific girl sessions on Friday evenings in Queen's Park about three years ago.

Chesterfield Girls took part in a competition (I cannot remember the name of the competition, but there is a trophy in the Pavilion) in 2007 and we won the trophy for Derbyshire and went to the next leg of the knock-out which was regional, but we didn't get through. We were however, very proud of ourselves because we hadn't played as a team before (we had played with a mixture of boys and girls at Chesterfield, but not all girls together). (Laura Slater)

Ladies have played an important part in the cricket in Queen's Park since 1889 when they raised £1,000 to pay for the field which was turned into the cricket ground.

Just after the First World War the park keeper's wife, Mrs Jenkinson, was paid £3 for the use of her rooms in South Lodge during the three county matches during the year which was increased to £4 10s., to the 'old standard', and later to £6. This was in the days when the Gentlemen and Players had separate accommodation.

In 1921, Mrs Middleton, wife of the groundsman, was paid 30s. for doing the washing.

Originally the Club provided all the kit which was transported to away matches in a big bag. Today the players have, and are responsible for, their own kit. However we have spare junior kit in all shapes and sizes so that no one need be deterred from playing because they haven't got the right kit. (Noëlle McCarroll)

I scored 150 against Beighton I think it was. I was getting weary and wondering when they were going to declare. I later found out that they were waiting for the tea to be got ready. In those days they had outside caterers. (George Lowe)

For Chesterfield matches there used to be four of us, mothers, wives and girlfriends, but not the same people every week. They used to get mugs of tea, sandwiches and cakes. (Margaret Walker)

Before the improvements to the pavilion we just did the teas for the Chesterfield games; for the two sides, scorers and umpires. It was hell! The pantry where the pans, crockery etc were stored was at the opposite end of the pavilion to the kitchen and there was a lot of walking to and fro and up and down steps. The kitchen was badly designed and, by today's standards, very unhygienic.

With the return of first-class cricket to Queen's Park, we have been given the opportunity to provide meals for the players and officials. This has been quite a challenge especially for the four-day games. Although it is hard work, we've thoroughly enjoyed ourselves. (Noëlle McCarroll)

A familiar figure in Queen's Park is Annette Owen, who is qualified to umpire Premier League and county second eleven games.

I was umpiring a game between Derbyshire and Nottinghamshire second elevens. It was a very hot August day and, as I was standing at the bowler's end, I was stung on the hand by a bee. Play was held up whilst I received treatment, but I think the physio was more concerned than I was. (Annette Owen)

43. Annette Owen looks on as Simon Lacey bowls. (Mike Taylor)

And yes there have been ladies playing cricket on the ground. In 1954 the Midlands (Women's Cricket Association) met New Zealand in a two-day game. Playing for the Midlands was Sheila Blyde of Rowsley, who captained Derbyshire against Leicestershire in July the same year in a one-day game. The weather was not kind. As the *Derbyshire Times* related:

> Women cricketers put up a performance on Saturday which should make the mere male cricketer blush with shame. Despite the atrocious weather the game between Derbyshire and Leicestershire was played to a finish. Six old men on seats near the stand, three men and a boy under the trees and a few friends in the shelter of the pavilion constituted the 'crowd' which watched Leicestershire take first knock in the pouring rain.

The weather did not deter Blyde who took eight wickets for 12 and then scored 24 out of the 49 Derbyshire required to win. In June 1971 it was the turn of Rachel Heyhoe's XI v The Rest of England XI.

Scorer for Chesterfield's First Eleven over the last 20 years has been Steve Franks:

> My earliest recollection of scoring a cricket match was from the television on a bit of scrap paper. The match was England versus Pakistan at The Oval in 1974 with Zaheer Abbas scoring 240.
>
> A few years later I started scoring properly for Clowne Phoenix, my local club, who played in the North Derbyshire League. I cannot remember ever having been taught to score; I have picked it up by watching my fellow scorers.
>
> After Clowne Phoenix folded in 1987 I was snapped up by Chesterfield Cricket Club; the club's fixture secretary at the time, Peter Kirk, worked in the same office as me. One of my first matches was at Steetley when Dean Hopkinson (113 including one six and 12 fours), and Harry Cartwright (131 including two sixes and 20 fours), put on 268 for the first wicket in 46 overs. This game really brought home the level of cricket I was now involved in. Chesterfield's number three batsman, making his debut for the club, was Derbyshire professional Tim O'Gorman — he never got a bat!
>
> Over the years at Chesterfield I have adapted my scoring style so that I can record the number of balls faced. I currently score using a linear method adapted so that I can use the standard scorebook.
>
> Normally I score for first team games and the opposition scorer and myself sit in the score box, which can be very cold on a miserable day in April and boiling hot on a mid-summer's day. I

prefer not to score behind glass as in that way you can hear more of what is happening on the field and feel part of the game. We also have to operate the scoreboard itself.

When I first joined the club the results were telephoned in to a results service and a results sheet with all match details completed and posted to the League Fixture Secretary. The League Press Secretary contacted the clubs on Sundays for details of First Division matches. Now deadlines are much tighter, basic details have to be rung into the League so that they can be available for the papers and Ceefax by 10 p.m. on the night of the match. The full match details have to be entered onto an online results service, the Play-Cricket website run by ECB, by the Wednesday following the game on Saturday. (Steve Franks)

Scorer for the Second Eleven is Noëlle McCarroll who, like Steve, inputs the results to the Play-Cricket web site. When Derbyshire played their Twenty20 warm up games in the Park she scored for the Chesterfield Invitation XIs alongside Derbyshire's scorer, John Brown.

7 First-class cricket returns

The establishment of the Heritage Lottery Fund gave a lifeline to public parks in general. The application by the Borough Council for money from the Fund to restore Queen's Park was successful in 2003 and work began the following year. In the pavilion the changing-rooms were moved upstairs and a room for community use established downstairs.

At the same time Chesterfield Cricket Club sought funds from the England and Wales Cricket Board. The planned increase in coaching for youngsters played an important part of the application for funding. A grant was received from their Community Club Development Fund of £55,000 for the renovation of the 21 strips forming the square and the improvement of practice facilities. Two artificial strips were laid on the turf in front of the scoreboard and a third, with a permanent cage, and which can be used at any time, was laid adjacent to the scoreboard.

The MCC awarded a first-class match to Queen's Park in 2002 when a strong MCC side, including Derbyshire's Kevin Dean, played the Sri Lankans.

44. Edwin Smith surveys the scene during the Chesterfield v Derbyshire Twenty20 game in 2005. (Chesterfield Borough Council)

The pavilion was completed in time for a belated start to the 2005 cricket season. Derbyshire County Cricket Club returned in June for two practice matches and a Second Eleven match in glorious weather and in front of big crowds. Derbyshire were happy, the Council was happy and in July 2006 first-class cricket returned to Queen's Park. It was a very emotional day for the cricket fans.

> It was good when first-class cricket came back. Although I have meetings with the Derbyshire groundsman he mostly lets me get on with the job reasoning that I know the most about the pitch. It is a quick-drying pitch but with clay soil it does tend to dry out and crack in the summer. (Tim Nicholls)

> It must have been fate that my first year on the First-class Umpires list, 2006, was also the year that county cricket returned to Queen's Park.
>
> It was Derbyshire versus Worcestershire and John Steele and I were appointed to umpire the match. The weather was superb, the cricket good, and the hospitality laid on for us was quite outstanding in the newly refurbished pavilion.
>
> My one real memory of the match was having to give Michael Di Venuto run out from a direct hit by Vikram Solanki after a fine innings of 99.
>
> I then umpired the Pro 40 match following the Championship game on the Sunday where Surrey were the visitors. Queen's Park was packed to capacity and it was a great sight. Surrey ran out comfortable winners, again on a superb pitch.
>
> So I have many happy memories of the beautiful ground that is Queen's Park and I hope that in future years I will be appointed to many more matches there, because being a first-class umpire means I tend to spend a lot of time away in the summer and not only is Queen's Park one of my favourite grounds, it is also the nearest to home on the south side of Sheffield. (Richard Kettle-borough)

During the 1950s the County Club and the Council jointly funded the construction of the terraces to the west of the pavilion and the press-room and score-box at the back of them. Later a new press-room and score-box was built adjacent to the pavilion. During the restoration this was in turn replaced by brick-built accommodation, much to the delight of the scorers.

> When I heard that Derbyshire were returning to play first-class cricket Queen's Park in the 2006 season, I was delighted. It is one of

45. The crowd gathers round the newly restored pavilion for the Graeme Welch benefit match in June 2007. (Janet Murphy)

the most beautiful grounds in the country, and one on which I had always hoped that I would be able to score for the County.

I had scored there once, although unofficially, as the computer scorer for the Press Association when the MCC played against the Sri Lankan tourists in 2002. Then I had sat with the press in their open-fronted, green-painted press box alongside the pavilion. The information which I recorded on the computer travelled through the ether to Yorkshire from where it was quickly transmitted (within 30 seconds) for teletext and the internet, and this still happens when I am scoring for all home matches.

Since that match six years ago a great deal of work had been done on the ground, especially in and around the pavilion. The press box has gone and a new room had been built in its place for the scorers. In here there is plenty of space and a good-sized worktop — essential for scorers who are keeping the score on laptops as well as in large hard-backed scorebooks.

There is a good view of the play, although at first preoccupied spectators had to be asked to move away from our window, since it provided a good meeting point for people wanting a drink and a chat. Since this area has been blocked off to the public, the view is perfect and the umpires are clearly able to see our acknowledge-ments to their signals. In addition I have two walkie-talkies, one to speak with the umpires and one with the scoreboard operators.

A great advantage for the scorers is that the pavilion is so close: at Derby the scorers have to walk across the ground at the lunch interval, so the afternoon session is always accompanied by shortage of breath and indigestion. The twenty-minute tea interval is too short even for this walk, so we rely on a tray of sandwiches carried round the boundary by the dressing room attendant. At Chesterfield, already renowned for the excellence and generosity of its catering, the scorers walk barely a pitch-length to join the queue for their lunch and tea.

I was very pleased to see that the fixture-planners had doubled the number of days at Queen's Park for the 2008 season. I think this is a well-deserved expansion for the committee and workers at the club, one which deserves fine weather and success, not only off the field, but on it as well. Yes, I am still waiting to record a win for Derbyshire at Chesterfield — surely 2008 will be the year! (John Brown)

When the fixtures were published for 2007 there was a pleasant surprise for Ian Blackwell.

46. Keeping the listeners up to date, David Jepson of Radio Derby and Jim Brailsford in the commentary box. (Mike Taylor)

I had a welcome surprise when the Somerset fixtures came through, Derbyshire v Somerset at Queen's Park! What were the odds on that? I'm very much looking forward to playing there, albeit in a Somerset shirt. (Ian Blackwell)

It was not to be. Heavy rains left the park flooded and the pitch waterlogged. The matches were transferred to Derby. Instead the festival games were played in September, once more in glorious weather. Taking advantage of a lightning fast out-field, the Nottinghamshire captain Stephen Fleming stroked his way to 243 off 264 balls. For Derbyshire there was some consolation as Jonathan Clare took five wickets for 90 runs, the first player to take five wickets in an innings on his Derbyshire debut for 25 years.

8 Last words

Sadly Les Jackson died in 2007. A service of thanksgiving for his life was held at St Mary's and All Saints — the Crooked Spire — on the eve of what should have been the start of the cricket festival. After the service some of his former team mates attended a buffet in the cricket pavilion in Queen's Park. What memories that must have evoked.

47. Peter Eyre marks out his run up just as he did when he took six for 18 in the Gillette Cup Semi-final in 1969. (Mike Taylor)

The affection with which Queen's Park is regarded by players, spectators and officials alike is evident from people's memories of cricket in the Park.

> Queen's Park, Chesterfield is steeped in history, home of great cricketing legends, and some wonderful cricket matches have been played there. I have some wonderful memories which I shall always treasure: memories which money cannot buy. Queen's Park will always be so dear to my heart as a player and umpire. (Dickie Bird)

> Queen's Park is a fantastic ground and will always hold a special place in my heart. (Ian Blackwell)

But the last word goes to an ordinary club cricketer.

> I only played on the Park twice. Once for Boythorpe Youth Club in the final of the Hill Trophy, i.e. 20-overs-a-side, we lost, and once in

48. The President of Derbyshire County Cricket Club, Nick Owen, together with former players after the Les Jackson Memorial Service. *Standing:* Peter Gibbs, Harry Cartwright, Jim Brailsford, Edwin Smith, Peter Eyre. *Seated:* Bob Taylor, Nick Owen, Donald Carr and Derek Morgan. (Mike Taylor)

adult life when I played for Chesterfield NALGO team against Chesterfield Third Eleven in a friendly very early on in April 1955. We drew the match but the memory for me was having tea in the pavilion and thinking about the famous players who had had their teas there, Don Bradman, Len Hutton, the list is endless. (Ken Silcock)

Contributors

Brian Austin, Clive Baxter, Dickie Bird, Ian Blackwell, John Bolton, Andy Bowers, Trevor Bowring, Dougie Brown, John Brown, Ian Buxton, Harry Cartwright, Michael Cole, John Cook, Ray Farnsworth, Steve Franks, Peter Gibbs, David Griffin, Roger Hartley, Brian Jackson, Chris Jaques, Peter Joy, Tim Kemp, Richard Kettleborough, Charlie Lee, Tommy Leonard, W. Leverton, George Lowe, Noëlle McCarroll, Steve McCarroll, Mrs Mallender, Geoff Miller, John Morris, Tim Nicholls, Tim O'Gorman, Fran O'Neill, Annette Owen, Tony Pope, John Redhead, Harold Rhodes, Ken Roe, Phil Russell, David Short, Ken Silcock, Ben Slater, Laura Slater, Edwin Smith, Richard Suttle, Mike Taylor, Margaret Walker, Colin Wilbourne

Illustrations

Trevor Bowring, Jim Brailsford, Chesterfield Borough Council, Chesterfield Cricket Club, Chesterfield Library Local Studies, Chesterfield Museum and Art Gallery, Colin Clewes (Cricket New South Wales), *Derbyshire Countryside*, the *Derbyshire Times*, Peter Joy, George Lowe, Mrs Mallender, Noëlle McCarroll, MCC Photo Library, Pat Pick, Tony Pope, Raymond Photographic Agency, Ken Roe, Mrs Rogers, *Sheffield Telegraph and Star*, John Smith (Chesterfield Borough Council), Mike Taylor, D. Tyler.